jaded faith

hope for those who still want to believe

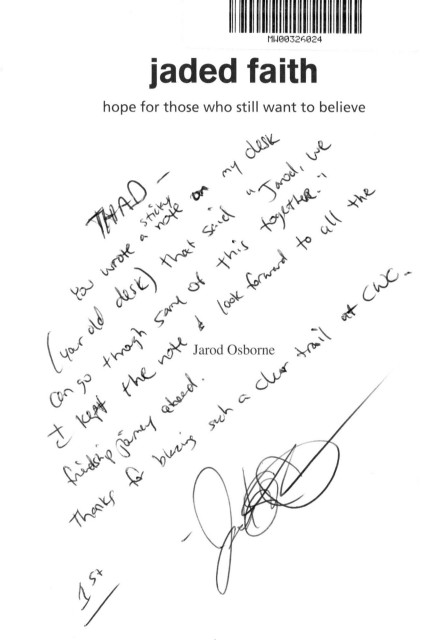

THAD —

You wrote a sticky note on my desk (your old desk) that said "Jarod, we can go through some of this together." I kept the note & look forward to all the friendship journey ahead.

Thanks for blazing such a clear trail at CWC —

Jarod Osborne

1st

wph wesleyan
publishing
house

Indianapolis, Indiana

Copyright © 2012 by Jarod Osborne
Published by Wesleyan Publishing House
Indianapolis, Indiana 46250
Printed in the United States of America
ISBN: 978-0-89827-570-4

Library of Congress Cataloging-in-Publication Data

Osborne, Jarod.
 Jaded faith : hope for those who still want to believe / Jarod Osborne.
   p. cm.
 ISBN 978-0-89827-570-4
 1. Young adults--Religious life. 2. Christian life. 3. Christianity and culture.
 I. Title.
 BV4529.2.O83 2012
 248.4--dc23
                                        2012029235

All Scripture quotations, unless otherwise indicated are taken from the HOLY BIBLE, NEW INTERNATIONAL VERSION®. Copyright © 1973, 1978, 1984 by the International Bible Society. Used by permission of Zondervan. All rights reserved.

Scripture quotations marked (NLT) are taken from the *Holy Bible, New Living Translation*, copyright 1996, 2004. Used by permission of Tyndale House Publishers, Inc., Wheaton, Illinois 60189. All rights reserved.

For those who have been jaded but are not ready to give up

contents

Acknowledgements 7

1. Meltdown 9

2. Narrow Path 17

3. Dull Church 31

4. Hypocrites 47

5. Pain and Suffering 61

6. Rationalism 85

7. Evolution 107

8. Relativism 127

9. The Other Reason 147

10. Moving Forward
    with Life 153

acknowledgements

A book is always a community event. Many people have influenced me and this work. The subject matter of this book has played itself out in real-time in my life. Sometimes it was ugly, unnerving, even dangerous.

I want to thank my family for training me in the way I should walk. I will not stray from it. I appreciate my close friends, especially Matt who has shown me the meaning of loyalty. I am thankful for great mentors who have motivated me to keep moving forward with life and writing, especially Keith Drury. I am grateful to those at Wesleyan Publishing House for their desire to ignite a passion for God and their willingness to take a risk with a young writer whose faith was once jaded. I want to thank each person who examined this work in its early stages and offered vital feedback toward its development. I am thankful for my wife, Esther, who is more than I deserve. And I also want to thank you, the reader, for being interested in this book, for ingesting it, and for investing hope into others.

It's a good thing to have all
the props pulled out from
under us occasionally.
It gives us some sense of
what is rock under our feet,
and what is sand.

—Madeleine L'Engle

1

meltdown

sooner or later

"Sooner or later everyone becomes jaded."

He stood in the parking lot with his friends, acting like he had the world figured out. As he made his fatalistic declaration, his face revealed he was already jaded. The bright summer day dimmed slightly at his hopeless words.

I had a sudden urge to grab the guy by the collar, meet him eye to eye, and say, "Fine, maybe everyone does get jaded. Then what?" Instead, I said nothing. I kept on walking. I let him have the last word.

He and his buddies got in their car and drove away. But his words remained like acid on my skin. I wish I had said something to counter his cynicism. I was silent then, but not anymore.

options and promises

We have a dizzying array of options. We can pick from hundreds of pairs of shoes, dozens of cereals, and millions of songs. There are all kinds of people we might choose to befriend or date. There are many variations of floor plans and locations of homes to buy, build, or rent. Our entertainment options are almost unlimited. To prove the point, visit a developing nation for a week or two. Stay in a remote village. You'll learn the meaning of limited options.

Not only do we have a variety of options, but we also have flexibility to change our minds if we're not happy with our first choice. Don't like the TV show you're watching? Change the channel. Bored with your girlfriend or boyfriend? Find another one. And if you decide you don't like the sweater you just bought, return it for a full refund.

Many of us shuffle through our options as if we're searching a deck of cards for an ace. Advertisements promise fulfillment. Our desire for happiness leads us from one option to the next. And still we can't seem to find what we're looking for.

This is what it means to be jaded.

It is to be dulled by overindulgence and wearied by overexposure, overstimulation, and overuse. Our high expectations are smashed. We rekindle our hope for another attempt only to be disappointed again. We become burned-out skeptics, especially when it comes to religion, the largest marketer of hope. Christianity makes the biggest promises. And perhaps yields the biggest disappointments.

sunday school dropouts

Many people grow up hearing Bible stories in church. They're excited to be in the "Lord's army." That is, until they hit the war. Then they realize their basic training didn't prepare them for what was ahead. Facing the challenges of adulthood, they find the deep well of their religion to be unexpectedly dry. They become Sunday school dropouts, soldiers gone AWOL. They say:

• Where was God when I needed him?
• Where's the happiness I was promised?
• Why didn't God answer my prayers?
• Everyone knows science contradicts the Bible.
• Christians are all fakes and backstabbers.
• The church just wants my money.

If the Christian faith promises so much, why are so many people abandoning ship? Why, according to *USA Today*, are one-fourth of Protestant Christians leaving the church as young adults?[1] They give many reasons, such as:

• I'm too busy.
• It doesn't fit my work schedule.
• It isn't a priority for me.
• I don't see the need.
• I moved away to college.
• I'm taking a break from organized religion.

There is, however, a deeper reason. It's like a shadow over our souls: We are a jaded generation. Considering all the hurts, broken promises, doubts, and confusion, trusting God might not seem like the best option. After all, there are many other choices. But losing hope in God feels like you're being betrayed by your first love. The one you trusted broke your heart. And when you've lived through a break-up, it's harder to give your heart away the next time.

outside looking in

Then there are those who never did the Sunday school thing. They didn't grow up in a Christian family. These people are on the outside looking in. The "product" never disappointed them because they never purchased it in the first place. Still, they know they need something. They know there is an important search taking place. They know God is one option. But they're still punching keywords into the search engines of their souls, trying to find the best match. They, too, have a thousand reasons to be skeptical about Christianity. They have their own intellectual quandaries. They've heard the horror stories. They've probably dealt with the collateral damage from church fights. Maybe they think it's best to avoid that road altogether. Maybe with God it's really not better to have loved and lost than to have never loved at all.

who's writing this?

I know you're not going to trust me until you know I've suffered. Even then, you might be hesitant. There was a time when I refused to listen to anyone unless they had scars. I vomited up the prepackaged answers I had been spoon-fed my whole life. I was starving for something that could survive the assault of my doubts and questions. I wanted more than a spiritual sugar high.

When I was a teenager, I was absolutely devoted to Jesus. I memorized Bible verses, prayed fervently, and told others about the plan of salvation. I had a Christian family, and my faith in God was ingrained in me since childhood. I went to a private school. I was the role model leader in my youth group. I taught weekly Bible studies in my home. Strenuous fasting was a regular part of my lifestyle. My family was very active in our church.

I entered college to study Christian ministry with the intention of being a pastor. I was confident. I knew God had called me to ministry. I had the answers. I knew where to find the Bible verses. I was on fire.

Half-way through college, everything changed. The events of my life aligned to create the perfect storm. The downpours put out my fire. First, someone I trusted broke my heart. This caused me to question God's love for me. Then I began traveling the world. The strangeness of other cultures and their ways of thinking brought serious doubts about my beliefs. This sent me in a tailspin of anger and confusion. My secure life was shaken. Inside I yearned for answers.

I started to search. I wanted to know what was true, and I wanted to experience it firsthand. I needed to see if my childhood religion could stand up against the cruel realities of the world. So I began my vision quest. I packed my emotional, spiritual, and physical bags, and became a sort of wanderer. I sojourned through cities and wilderness. I visited some of the world's poorest people. I tested my strength in the fighting ring. I tackled my rational entanglements with renowned scholars. I sat under monks and vagabonds. I slept on the street with the homeless and in the luxury suites of the wealthy. For nearly a decade, I screamed and cursed and wandered. My confident answers had bled into a murky pool of doubts. My faith was demolished. I abandoned the ministry. I didn't know who I would become or what I would believe.

I was jaded.

I almost did not survive this journey. I lingered at forks in the road that, if I had chosen the wrong way, would have ruined me. But I refused to give up. I believed there had to be more to life than brokenness. I decided that I did not want to remain in a jaded state. I didn't want to be defined by what I was walking away from, but by what I was pursuing.

hope ahead

I can appreciate skeptics. I was one for a long time. Being a skeptic often means that you're searching for truth with grit and resolve. You're not satisfied with cheap substitutes or somebody else's opinions. You sift carefully through the sand, straining out rocks and garbage. That kind of honesty is admirable. What is not admirable is quitting. You don't have to be destroyed by difficult circumstances, to admit defeat prematurely, to dwell on the negative, or to give up on life while you're still breathing. That's not honesty; it's a tragedy.

Who knows? Maybe the guy in the parking lot was right. Maybe sooner or later everyone becomes jaded. But I am interested in what can happen after that.

note

1. Cathy Lynn Grossman, "Young Adults Aren't Sticking with Church," *USA Today*, August 6, 2007, http://www.usatoday.com/news/religion/2007-08-06-church-dropouts_N.htm.

You have brains in your head.
You have feet in your shoes. You
can steer yourself any direction
you choose. You're on your
own. And you know what you
know. And *YOU* are the [one]
who'll decide where to go.

—**Dr. Seuss**

2

narrow path

the wrong path at sundown

We raced into the office five minutes before closing. The park ranger was visibly annoyed that we arrived so close to the end of her shift.

"Can we get a backcountry permit please?" I politely asked, trying to smooth out her frustration.

"Yes, but your options are limited," she said as she pulled out a park map. We chose a campsite in the remote southwest corner of the park. She issued our permit and handed me a single sheet of white paper with a map printed on it.

"Walk straight into the canyon, and you'll find your campsite right here." Her finger touched the map. It looked easy. The map was simple. We thanked her and hurried to the trailhead.

I led; my wife followed me. Zion's beauty was more stunning than I had imagined of a desert landscape. This trail was not like the hardened dirt of the Appalachians. Little specks of sand kicked up with every step. Distant mountains loomed in all directions. Not a cloud to separate us from the blue sky. And silence. Our quiet sandy steps and the gentle rustle of weeds were the only sounds for miles.

We got a late start, so a hint of urgency bled through our steps. Armed with a generic map, we entered the canyon. Within a few miles, a ranger passed us by. He was the only other person we saw on the trail. As he waved, a tiny voice inside told me to ask him about our campsite. "Are we going the right way?" I wanted to say. "How much farther?" But I just waved back and walked on.

Esther followed me into the shadow of the narrowing mountains. But her anxiety grew as she realized we had come to a fork in the path. Several little trails branched off, and there were no signs to guide us. Our bird's-eye-view map offered no help. And it was sundown.

Now with quickened pace, we chased down the path farther into the canyon. No—it was the wrong way. Then we retraced our steps and took the other fork in the road, up the mountain. It was a taxing climb, especially since we didn't know if we were going in the right direction. This path led to another divergence. So we tried one way, then another. The last rays of sunlight were melting away, and we were running out of time. Just then, we spotted it: campsite 3. After breathing a sigh of relief, we set our backpacks down and took a look around. Our campsite was on the rim of the canyon, overlooking miles of rusty mountains and a breathtaking drop to the river below. The view was spectacular! Zion was an apt name. This spot was worth all the sweating and fretting.

This hike reminded me of the critical importance of two things—a knowledgeable guide and a good map.

embarked on a journey

Our lives are going somewhere. We are embarked on a journey simply by being born. The paths we choose will determine our destinies. The burning question is, "Where am I going?" Take a look at the people around you, especially older adults. Their lives end up in different places. Some people are wealthy, while others are poor. Some are crotchety complainers, while others are gentle sages. Some end their lives surrounded by loving family; others are buried in loneliness and regret. Why does one person's life inspire us, while another's wounds us? Why are some who die heralded as heroes and others as "a sad story"?

The difference is the paths they chose. They took one little step after another, and it led them to a destination. Jesus spoke about paths. "For wide is the gate and broad is the road that leads to destruction, and many enter through it. But small is the gate and narrow the road that leads to life, and only a few find it" (Matthew 7:13–14).

He wasn't just talking about geographical locations. This path is about your whole life, and it involves every part of you—body, mind, heart, soul, relationships—everything. And according to Jesus, most people are on the wrong path. They are going the wrong direction. Where does the broad path lead? To destruction. That path leads off a cliff. To doom. To bodily harm. To spiritual disaster. To relational breakdown. To mental distress. The most well-traveled path is headed to death. And yet most people are daily plodding toward destruction.

The narrow path, however, leads somewhere else—to life! To wholeness and goodness in every area of your being. This life never ends. But the path is not obvious. Most people have missed it.

So how are we to find it?

An expert guide is essential. It's as if Jesus is issuing an urgent trail advisory to all hikers, saying, "Watch out! There are many paths to choose from. The easiest and more populated ones are fatal. If you follow them, you won't make it back alive. But there is a beautiful, challenging, rewarding, little path that cuts through all the disasters and leads you to your ultimate destination. I can guide you on this path. I know it well, and if you follow me, I'll make sure you're OK."

false sense of security

It would have been foolish for me to try to comfort my wife by saying, "Don't worry honey. I don't know where we're going, but it doesn't matter. All these paths will eventually lead us to our campsite." The truth is, the other paths did not lead to our campsite. Only one did. Despite my best words of consolation, what we really needed was to find the right path.

Many in our culture have been singing themselves to sleep with a deceptive lullaby. They say with gentleness and sincerity that it doesn't matter which road you travel. They say every belief system will eventually lead you to God. In other words, we hear that all paths lead to the campsite. This is nonsense. Literally. It makes no sense. All paths are not the same, nor do they lead in the same direction. Neither is it enough just to enjoy the journey. If you were in a canoe that was about to plummet over a deadly waterfall, would you sit back and enjoy the ride or try to change course? Jesus is trying to advise us. There is a road that leads to life. Few find it, so pay close attention.

doubts and questions

Jesus is our expert guide. We're lost without him. We are going the wrong way, and it will destroy us. Our hope and our lives depend upon following him. We also have an essential navigation tool for the journey—the Bible.

To a jaded generation, talking about Jesus and the Bible stirs up an array of doubts and questions. I don't expect you to swallow it whole. In fact, you're probably reading this book because you have some serious issues with Christianity, doubts about Jesus, or questions about the Bible. Is it OK to question God? Is it OK to ask God questions? Is it OK to question and doubt what you're taught? Sure.

God wants us to know and love him with our intellect, experience, emotions, and decisions. This involves some honest exploration. It is good to question. It probably means you're searching for truth. God likes it when we search for truth, because he is truth. He knows that a search for reality will ultimately lead us to the narrow path. And that path will lead us to life. Jesus even said, "I am the way and the *truth* and the life" (John 14:6, emphasis added). If we seek God, really look for him intently, we will find him. Questions fuel this quest.

no help at all

I accepted Jesus when I was six years old. I was baptized several years later. I was devoted to God at a very young age. But in high school, I encountered some passages in the Bible that seemed to contradict one another. This threw me into a tailspin. I had put my unyielding faith in the truth of the Bible as God's word. There had to be some way to reconcile the contradictions.

After church one Sunday, I charged into my youth pastor's office, Bible in hand. I laid out my questions like a math problem, expecting him to retort with the solution. Instead, he said, "Yeah, those are good questions." We discussed the problems but never came to the solutions.

Our conversation quelled a portion of my anxiety, but it did nothing to untangle my intellectual conundrums. So I put the questions on the back burner for a while.

A few years later, while in college, similar questions and doubts arose. My whole life I had been living for Jesus. And now I had some honest questions about the whole thing. I wanted some honest answers. Was that too much to ask? I knocked on the door of a different pastor this time. Like watching a bad movie twice, I laid out my concerns and frustrations expecting some guidance. His answers only exacerbated my questions. I left the office once again shoving my doubts to the back burner. But the heat was rising. These were educated, loving, spiritual pastors. They had my best interest in mind. They took my concerns seriously. But their words did not arrest my slide down the mountain of doubts toward the cliff of despair.

dreams and lists

My friend experienced hurtful events earlier in her life that caused her to question God. She wanted to know why God would allow pain and frustration to crash down on her for no apparent fault of her own. During this period of struggle, she dreamed that she died. She stood outside the gates of heaven with a scroll in her hands. On the scroll, she had written all her questions for God. She intended to march up to God and read her list and get some solid answers. But then she was escorted into heaven. The streets glimmered in her wide eyes. She saw colors for which she had no name. And then she heard a beautiful noise. Angels and people singing to their eternal audience—God. Without a thought, she dropped the scroll and opened her mouth—not to ask questions, but to join in the song.

This dream reminds me of an ancient story in the Bible about a man named Job. The writer went out of his way to let us know that Job was a good man. He did not deserve to be punished. But calamity struck, and Job's happy life was broken. His children were killed. His wealth was eliminated. He even lost his health. So he was left with his deteriorating body, his wife who told him to curse God, and a few friends who told him he was being punished by God. Job did nothing wrong, and he became mad. He questioned God. Read these words from Job 23:2–9:

My complaint today is still a bitter one, and I try hard not to groan aloud. If only I knew where to find God, I would go to his court. I would lay out my case and present my arguments. Then I would listen to his reply and understand what he says to me. Would he use his great power to argue with me? No, he would give me a fair hearing. Honest people can reason with him, so I would be forever acquitted by my judge. I go east, but he is not there. I go west, but I cannot find him. I do not see him in the north, for he is hidden. I look to the south, but he is concealed. (NLT)

Job wanted to put God on trial. He wanted to read his list of questions and complaints before God, and get a straight answer. Job did receive an answer, but it was not what he expected.

So, maybe a list is a good place to start. Creating a list of questions for God is a form of prayer. It is an acknowledgement that our pain is real. It is a way of bringing our difficulties to God and asking for help, instead of running away from him. It shows that we are not willing to ignore the problems but work through them. It says we want something more than to be beaten down by life's doubts and pain. We want answers and hope, and we are willing to search for them. Questions fuel the quest.

creating a list

Sometimes while talking with people, I discover they are atheistic or agnostic. When I ask why they don't believe in God, they say something like, "There are just too many problems with Christianity," or "I have a lot of unanswered questions."

I then ask, "Will you explain your questions to me?" What usually follows is a mostly inarticulate attempt to defend their unbelief. Many people who say they have doubts and questions cannot clearly explain either. They carry around vague concepts or past wounds as their defenses for not having faith.

When I was having a faith meltdown, I began to clarify the key issues that were melting down. This list helped me focus on what it was that really troubled me. It also gave me a direct line of communication with God. I knew what I was praying about and what I needed help with.

My list looked something like this:

1. Why does God allow pain and tragedy to happen to those who love him (specifically me!)?

2. Do people really go to hell and burn forever? If so, why would God do that to anyone?

3. If Jesus is the "only way" to life, how am I supposed to relate to my non-Christian friends?

4. If there is one truth, why are there so many different religions in the world?

5. Does God love the poor, hungry, and homeless? If so, why does he let them stay that way?

6. Is my faith in God based on my material blessings? Would I still believe if they disappeared?

7. How could God let me think my former girlfriend was "the one," when she just ended up breaking my heart?

8. Why does the Bible apparently contradict science, reason, and even itself?

This list was the hinge joint of the mess. I knew that if any Christian teacher was going to speak to me, they better have something meaningful to say about these issues. These questions were the fodder for my angry prayers. They were the wounds and fears that made me jaded in the first place. To find hope was to navigate through them. I was no longer willing to avoid the questions or skirt around them. No more back burner. The questions had reached their boiling point.

What are your questions? Do you desire to live life to the fullest? Do you want hope to emerge from your fog of doubts? Are you looking for what is true? If you are, then do it right.

Get serious. Don't just walk carelessly down the broad road. You know where that leads. Search desperately for the narrow road. Fight for your life because that is what is at stake.

You can begin by carefully crafting a list of your questions and concerns. What do you want to ask God? What seems to be tripping you up in your spiritual journey? Take a few minutes to write your ideas in a journal or someplace that you will see often.

a bit of good news

If you are serious about finding God, then you need to know that he is already pursuing you. He has been crazy about you from before you were born. He loves you; he desires for you to have the best life possible. That's why he made you in the first place. He cares about your pain and frustrations, and he is eager to lead your life if you are willing to follow.

Even if you are not searching for him, he still loves you. Even if you're glad to be on the broad road, God is still pursuing you with affection. He wants what is best for you, and only he can lead you to it. In fact, God is what is best for you!

Maybe you don't believe in God. Perhaps you're not convinced that there is any hope. That's OK. Start asking God your questions, and you've begun the journey to full life. You may be thinking, "But how can I ask God my questions when I don't believe that he exists?" Begin talking to God, even if you don't believe in him. This will show him that you are willing to believe he could exist. And that's a good start.

If you are committed to believing that there is no God, hope, or grace out there, then you can close the book now. Our paths have diverged. However, if there's a shred of hope in your heart that there might be some meaning to life, and you're willing to explore it, then we have a journey ahead of us.

a bit more good news

You're not in this alone. Many pioneers have gone before you on this quest. They are those who found the narrow path and followed its course. They were not disappointed. There are others who are journeying right now. I'm one of them. We are in this together.

Smart people have asked questions just like yours. Good-hearted people have faced challenges similar to yours. Strong people have been wounded like you have. Some have chosen to give up on life and walk the broad path, but others have kept following the expert guide.

If you take the risk to get serious about searching for God, you will immediately notice that you've taken the road less traveled. Jesus warned us that the broad road is where most people go. The crowd doesn't know where they're going, so don't be surprised if they question where you go. If you are looking for good reasons not to follow Jesus, you'll find them. If you are looking for friends to walk the broad road with, you'll find them. But if you're looking for life, you'll find it. And you'll be among friends. I'll walk with you through each chapter. Consider also finding another friend who will read and discuss this book with you. Or perhaps you can ask your questions with a group of like-minded people.

where this book leads

We are going to face six core, crisis issues of our time. These six cause many travelers to leave the narrow path or never walk it in the first place. Some try to avoid these issues, walking miles out of their way to bypass them. Others come face-to-face with them and then turn back. We are going to go through them and come out the other side. The six issues are: dull church, hypocrites, pain and suffering, rationalism, evolution, and relativism. There is also another reason I'll address later.

As we begin this journey together, let me add a few things:

1. I am not writing about theories alone. I'm not writing because I have to. I'm writing this because I have been bloodied up on the side trails. I'm convinced that Jesus is the expert guide when it comes to living. We are lost without him, whether we know it or not. My wanderings have led me to the narrow path. And there is life there. I want you to know that there is a way beyond the cynicism of our culture. There's more to life than boring churches or blind chances. I want you to experience a better life.

2. This is hard. Life can hurt us. When we face the reality of our own situations, it may mean facing pain. When we meddle with the thoughts and experiences that gave birth to our questions, it may mean remembering things we'd rather forget. Fair warning: This journey is hard. Walking the narrow road

with Jesus is hard. Jesus repeatedly warned those who followed him that it would cost them everything. Are you ready to surrender everything?

3. Let's be honest. I'll be honest with you. You be honest with yourself. And give the journey an honest shot. If you take the time to reflect on the questions posed in these pages and work through the issues in your own heart, you'll have a better outcome.

4. This is about real life. We are discussing more than just ideas. This life journey involves everything that we are. Our whole selves. Don't think for a moment that it's just a philosophical sparring match. This is life and death.

5. You will encounter God. If you are open to God, he will show up. He'll surprise you. Remember, he's already pursuing you.

Some keep the Sabbath
going to Church—I keep
it, staying at Home.

—Emily Dickinson

3

dull church

dolls and mothballs

What comes to mind when you think about going to Grandma's house? What do you see? How do you feel? What do you smell?

I love my grandparents, and I always enjoy going to their homes. I have many great memories of visiting them, including the sight and smell of dolls (at my grandma's house) and mothballs (at my granny's house).

The dolls at my grandma's house were porcelain, fancy, stacked high in a showcase cabinet and on shelves. They were not the kind of dolls kids could play with. (Not that I would have played with them anyway!) I used to make a hobby of trying to count them. Every room was filled with them. I lost track somewhere around 140. I wonder how my grandma dusted all of them.

At Granny's house, the smell of the mothballs was strongest in the closet. My nose hasn't forgotten. It wasn't so much repelling as it was strange to me, almost endearing. As kids we identify people by their smells, by the feelings we get from being around them, and by their idiosyncrasies. Both the dolls and the mothballs were novelties.

Going to Grandma's house is like traveling to a foreign country. You encounter strange artifacts, like a typewriter or quilting frame. You're exposed to different kinds of food, like prunes. You might even have a language barrier. My granny was raised in the hills of Kentucky. Sometimes she would say a word that I couldn't understand, even though I knew it was in English. For example, all my life I heard my granny and mom talk about the annual gathering of their Old Regular Baptist Church. They called this meeting the "so-say-shun." I had no idea what this word meant. I just took it for granted. But a few years ago, my mom said the word *so-say-shun*. She doesn't have a Kentucky accent, and it sounded odd. A light bulb clicked on in my head.

"Oh!" I yelled. "The word is *association!*"

We paused for a moment, and then broke out into laughter. For years I had used the word without knowing what it meant.

grandma's church

When you think of going to church, what images come to mind?

For some going to church is similar to going to Grandma's house. It was fun as a kid, but now it's outdated. The décor is from the Great Depression. The carpet is ugly. The furniture is uncomfortable. Strange smells haunt the Sunday school classroom. Perhaps a different language is spoken there. Maybe you've been to a church that reads from the King James Version of the Bible. My granny is a die-hard KJV reader. To her, there is no other Bible. I understand and respect her opinion. But it is not mine. I am not moved by the Holy Spirit when I hear words like *thou*, *speaketh*, and *verily*. They confuse me. Churchgoers themselves can also be hard to interpret. Monday through Saturday, people don't use words like *sanctification*, *hedge of protection*, or *regeneration* in their conversations. But Sunday morning, theological vocabulary becomes fashionable.

They even have strange food. Church people routinely get together and eat bread (usually disappointingly small wafers or crusty cubes). They say this little piece of bread represents the body of their God. Does that mean God is tiny, dried-out, *Ha!* and hard to swallow? Then they drink micro-shots of grape juice and say it's the blood of their leader. All this seems very strange from the outside.

The problem goes deeper. Yes, some churches have outdated facilities. They may sing old songs too. They might have strange customs to an outsider. But what if a church is totally irrelevant? What if it doesn't connect to your life? It doesn't answer your questions. It doesn't speak to your situation. It doesn't help you find God. You don't fit in. You feel awkward. Then what? In some churches, it feels like you need to take a whole college course on theology, vocabulary, Bible, and dress code just to attend worship. It breaks my heart when people go to church looking for God but find religion. Some churches seem to think the most important things are rituals and rules. Sometimes it feels like church has nothing to do with real life.

our roots

As I get older, my appreciation for my grandparents grows. They are living links. Their roots reach deep into the past and connect my family's history with my family's future. They can tell stories of old that reveal myself to me. Their wisdom is hard-earned and valuable. I take strength in my heritage.

My great-grandfather was a hard worker. I never met him except through stories. He scratched a living from the dirt. His sweat put food on the table for his twelve children. They were poor, but they were proud. He did not accept charity, because he knew God had given him two strong hands to provide for his family. He met trials with courage. "There are no cowards in the Lord's army," he would often say. When I meet dangers and difficulties in my life, I remember the resolve of my great-grandfather.

My grandfather's example also motivates me. He worked one job for most of his adult life, building guardrail on the side of the road. He rose at four in the morning, often greeted by stiff muscles and throbbing back pain. His days were long, and the work was strenuous. During breaks, the crew would drink a half gallon of water and lay down on a hill to give their legs a rest.

My great-grandmother-in-law was the first person in my wife's family tree to become a Christian. She became ill in her hometown in Puerto Rico. The doctors said she was going to die, so they sent her home to finish her days with her family. But an evangelist named Osborne came to town. She begged her family to take her to Osborne's revival meeting. So they carried her there. During that meeting, she prayed, "God, if you are real and what this evangelist is saying is true, heal me. If you do, I will give you my life." Instantly, she felt electricity surge through her body. That night her family carried her home and waited for her to die. But she recovered. She gave her life to Christ and lived many more healthy years. She also passed on her faith to her children. That same faith now lives on in my wife, and we will pass it on to our children.

These people are important. Their stories shape my life. So I can tolerate the smell of mothballs and overlook the color of the carpet. It's a small inconvenience to be with the people who love me. Besides, one day my grandkids are going to look at my clothes and speech and think I'm old-fashioned. I hope they can see more in me than my appearance.

The church also has a rich legacy of grandparents. Men and women have gone before and have made the church what it is today. Some of our spiritual ancestors died for their faith. Some were put in prison. They had the courage to abandon the broad path and become leaders on the narrow way—no matter the cost. We dare not dismiss these great pilgrims because their clothes looked out of date.

The hymns that seem so ancient now were once edgy. The tired choruses from a generation ago were instrumental in forming people's lives. That old musty carpet was laid down years ago by a church member who sacrificially volunteered his time. That archaic Sunday school model was once a vital force in educating masses of poor child laborers and teaching them to read. The bread and grape juice ritual has served as a common link for two millennia—uniting Jesus with his people and uniting the church with each other. I am not the measure of all things. I will not pass quick judgment on a church just because it seems irrelevant to me.

branching out

We can learn to appreciate the faith of our ancestors, even if we don't dress or sing like them. And we don't have to collect dolls either. Instead, we can continue their legacy. They hand off the baton to us, and we run the next leg of the race.

A natural progression happens during our late teens, twenties, and thirties. We gain independence. We begin searching for our individual career paths. We make new friends that will last a lifetime. We move out of our parents' houses. We question what we were taught as children. This process helps us to establish ourselves as individuals.

It would be unwise to simply embrace everything our parents tell us. We should ask questions in order to gain deeper understanding. This matures our faith. However, some use independence as an opportunity to rebel. They do the opposite of what they were taught, simply because they can.

Branching out on your own is a time to sort through what you were given, and what you will keep. You're deciding which family traditions to continue and which ones to discard. You are able to sift through what you believe, how you spend your money, and how you use your time. You also decide whether you'll go to church. This sorting is good. It makes your faith your own. It matures you. It also makes you increasingly responsible for your choices.

Your music is different than your grandparents? Your clothing is different. So are your church preferences. That's fine. Your relationship with God may not look like someone else's. It has to be genuine to you.

what it's all about

Church is not about memorizing verses and eating stale pieces of bread. The Bible is not an electric fence to zap you into being moral. Christianity is not a religious creed or code of conduct. It is a story. Every little story on earth is a page in the one great story. The main characters are God and people, even you and me. And the good news is that there is good news! This isn't a tragedy that ends in despair. The Bible contains a true narrative riddled with danger, turmoil, adventure, and excitement. The ending is good. If we only see Christianity as dolls and mothballs, it's irrelevant. But if we can understand the story for ourselves, we can find out where we fit into it.

The story starts with God. He created the universe and all it contains. He formed the earth, spoke the sun and moon into existence, and flung the stars in their places. Then he breathed life into the first human beings, Adam and Eve. God loved all that he created. (Hold on . . . we'll talk about evolution in chapter 7.)

God especially loved Adam and Eve. He made a home for them in a lush garden, ripe with all kinds of delicious vegetation. He walked with them and gave them authority and responsibility to be managers over the earth and to take care of it on his behalf. He also gave them boundaries for their own good. He told them not to do one particular thing: eat from a certain tree, the Tree of Knowledge of Good and Evil.

Temptation seized Adam and Eve, and they chose to disobey their Maker. They ate the fruit. The consequences that followed are what always happens when disobedience causes us to walk the broad road: death and destruction. Sin entered the story. It was like a disease that infected humanity from the inside out. It influenced their decisions and destinies. Sin wreaked havoc on God's good world. But instead of destroying or abandoning his creation, God had a plan to save it from death.

This plan of salvation involved a man named Abraham. God told Abraham to leave his homeland and go to an unfamiliar place. This new territory was going to be a better land, and there he would have many descendents. God promised to bless Abraham and use him to be a blessing to the entire world.

Abraham's descendents grew into a large group of people called the Hebrews. They were eventually enslaved by an Egyptian pharaoh and held captive for hundreds of years. Then God called Moses to break them out of slavery and lead the Hebrews back to the good land that God had promised to Abraham. So Moses did. After fighting off the surrounding people groups, the Hebrews inhabited the Promised Land and established a nation called Israel.

God intended to have a special relationship with the nation of Israel. And like Abraham, God wanted the nation to be a light to the entire world. But sin was still causing problems on the earth, even among God's special nation. Though God created humanity so he could have a loving relationship with them, we failed to live up to his ways. We turned our backs on his goodness, like a generational curse separating father from child. But instead of removing humanity from the face of the earth, God did something drastic. He initiated his master plan: Jesus Christ.

If anyone wonders whether God cares, Jesus is the resounding answer. Yes! God placed his own Son in the middle of this broken planet so that he could heal it. Jesus became a teacher, a doctor of miracles, a mystery to scholars, and a scapegoat for evil. The political and religious leaders had Jesus killed by Roman crucifixion on charges of blasphemy and treason. His death served as a sacrifice to cover and remove the sins of humanity. In other words, Jesus took the consequences of our sins onto himself. Then three days after his death he was brought back to life. He spent some time with his closest friends then handed off the mission to them. Today, those who believe in Jesus are like the Hebrews. We are freed from being slaves to sin. Those who give their lives to Jesus become part of a great nation—the kingdom of God. Those who receive Jesus as the Son of God are forgiven and saved from the disastrous path humanity is marching on.

Christianity is a story about becoming the person you were designed to be. It is a reality of hope. It is an invitation to a better life. It is a story of love. God is alive and desperately wants you to know him. He wants to forgive your sins and make your heart clean. He is waiting for you to respond in faith. He will make you a new person and give you a mission to accomplish in the world. Then, when your life here is over, you will travel further. Just as Abraham set out for a better land, our true home is with Jesus, and he will personally welcome us there when we have completed our sojourn on the earth.

join the church?

Another way to say *church* is to say *God's family*. If you give your life to Jesus, turn from your sins, and follow him, you are a part of the church. You're a member of God's family. It's a family marked by love, purpose, belonging, and hope. And your membership doesn't expire when you do. You belong forever. Even death cannot stop the church. The life after this one is much better. No crying, struggling, war, heartbreak, death, or loneliness. Instead, radiant joy.

We all want to have joy and belong to a loving family. So, being a part of the church is relevant. We are the family of God. Sometimes the family is dull and boring. Sometimes we get off track or lose focus. Sometimes we are just plain jerks. But we are going in the same direction—toward God, love, and heaven. So should you join a local church? Should you get involved with a particular congregation? Of course! You belong. You're a part of the family. Don't you spend time with your blood relatives? What would your own family think if you never got together with any of them?

finding a church

If you belong to Jesus, you belong to his family—the church. But how do you find the right community of believers to regularly gather with? Maybe you're a part of a church that is dull. Or maybe you're looking for a church because you are searching for God. Finding the right church is an important task. Let's take a look at the process from several different perspectives.

1. I'm searching for something in my life. Maybe church can help.

If you are looking for God, truth, or good relationships, church is a great place to go. Even if you're not exactly sure what you're looking for, church can help. It's important that you find the right kind of church and that you get connected. Here are some criteria that might help:

- You feel comfortable and are warmly welcomed.
- You already know someone who goes there.
- It's within driving distance for you.
- There are people your age.
- The leaders seem to care about visitors and people who aren't yet Christians.
- The music connects with you.
- You are able to get involved in a small group for Bible study and discussion.
- You can share your questions and doubts and receive good feedback.
- You are learning about God through the Bible.
- Your spouse or kids (if applicable) like it too.

2. I'm a Christian, but I don't go to a church regularly.

Remember, if you belong to Jesus, you belong to the church. While finding the right church might not be simple, the fact that you should go is. The searching process might take a week or several months. But don't give up until you're convinced you've found the church where God wants you to be. You might want to:

- Pray that God shows you which church is the right one for you.
- Visit where your friends or family go to church.
- Make a list of churches you intend to visit in your area.
- Resist the pressure to go to any particular church for the wrong reasons.

- Find a church where you can grow spiritually through the worship service and small groups.
- Find a church that models and teaches the Bible, holy living, and missional outreach.
- Find a church where the preaching and teaching are relevant to you (and your family, if applicable).
- If you know where God is leading you, be obedient and follow.

3. I'm a Christian, but I don't like my church.

If you are devoted to Jesus, but really frustrated with your local church, ask yourself these questions.

- What are the good things about my church?
- What don't I like about my church?
- How many of these list items (from above) stem from an improper attitude within me?
- If I move churches, will I find these same problems? Will I take them with me?
- Do I respect my church's history, leaders, mission, and vision?
- Do I feel God leading me to stay at my church and bring new life and support?
- Does the pastor want me to stay and help bring change?
- Is it time for me to find another church?
- What kind of church am I looking for? Why am I looking for this kind of church?

It is possible that you might answer these questions and realize that the problem is inside of you. Every church has conflict between its people. Is that worth leaving over? No church will ever meet all your needs and preferences. If you go on a search for the perfect church, you'll never get connected anywhere.

It is also important to consider that your frustrations might be divine promptings to do something constructive. If you think the music is boring, join the band or choir and bring new energy. If you think the bulletins are outdated, ask how you could help improve them. If your church lacks a ministry to your age group, perhaps you could start one. But first, check with your pastor and leaders to make sure they connect with your ideas. Don't try to hijack the church in order to change its direction. However, if you have support from the leadership, go in God's power to bring renewal.

If you aren't willing to be a part of the team and bring positive change, at least determine that you won't gripe from the sidelines.

If it really is time for you to find another church, your exit strategy is critical. Let your final act of service to the church be to leave it with grace. Don't storm out and make a scene. Don't bad-mouth leaders. Don't air your complaints to the congregation. And don't just stop coming. Meet with the pastor or a staff member and share your concerns. Inform him or her of your love for the church and your reasons for leaving it.

The people you leave behind in one church will be your neighbors again in heaven. Build love; don't burn bridges.

discover together

The road to life is narrow, but not so narrow that you have to walk it alone. You can't walk it alone. We only discover true life together. I have been to dull churches. I've fallen asleep during the service. Some Sunday mornings I hated to get out of bed. But I've also been to churches that buzz with excitement, where it's obvious that God's Spirit is there. I wanted to arrive early and stay late. These kinds of churches moved me to love God and serve others. These churches brought life like nothing else could.

Somewhere out there, your local church is waiting. You belong there. It's not perfect, but it's good. You can grow there; you can serve there; you can have life to the fullest extent. Don't let a bad experience with a dull church disrupt you from walking the narrow path with God's family.

zombies in church

When your doubt is highest and your faith lowest, church is often the last place you want to be. You might even feel dishonest for going. But church is exactly where you need to be the most. When your faith is weak, surround yourself with the faith of your Christian friends. When you can't pray, let them pray on your behalf. When you don't have a song in your heart, stand together with those who do and say, "I may not be able to sing a joyful song today, but I am here, God. Let their songs count for me too."

Bring your questions to church. Be real in worship. Don't fake it. Show up, even if you sit through the sermon like a zombie. Keep walking your zombie corpse into church and stick with God's family. That's where you belong!

questions for reflection

What aspects of the spiritual life of your parents do you want to hold on to in your own life? What do you want to change?

How connected are you to a church right now?

questions for action

How will you bring more life and energy to your church?

After reading this chapter, do you sense that God is calling you to take a specific action step? What is it?

They are not
all saints
who use
holy water.

—English Proverb

4

hypocrites

a fence between

I have some friends who live next door to a church. A wooden fence is the only thing that separates them from it. One day I asked them why they don't attend that church or any other. They told me that they went for a while many years ago. But then they said in a solemn tone, "A church member said something mean about us behind our backs. So we stopped going."

This is yet another tragic example supporting the perception that the church is full of hypocrites. You've probably heard it before. Maybe you've even said it. The barrier that blocks many from walking that narrow path with Jesus is not a wooden fence. It's hypocrites in the church.

We expect more from Christians. They are supposed to be loving, patient, and kind. Christians bear the name of Christ. To be a Christian means to be a "little Christ." They represent Jesus on the ground, in our neighborhoods, at our schools. People intuitively know this, whether they are Christians or not. They know what a real Christian should look like, even if they don't think they've ever seen one. These high expectations are easily shot down when a Christian doesn't act lovingly. It's like a girl betraying her own sister. Or a soldier who shoots at his own army. Aren't Christians supposed to love others, not wound them?

name-calling

My heart goes out to those who have a bad experience at church. I'm angry that they were hurt. For God's people, love is the highest goal. It takes a lot of courage for a person to visit a new church. This alone is a remarkable step. Often people who visit a church are in the midst of great pain or searching. They poke their heads into a church to see if there's any hope offered there. And somebody bites off their heads. A church member makes a comment about what they are wearing. No one asks their names or welcomes them with a smile. They are ignored by the clique that has been attending there for a decade. It doesn't take long for visitors to get the message that this is not a place to find love and hope. It doesn't always happen in church either. Christians can wound us at work, school, or even in our own homes.

If you've ever been burned by a hypocrite, you may be surprised to find that Jesus is more upset about hypocrisy than you are. See what he said:

What sorrow awaits you teachers of religious law and you Pharisees. Hypocrites! For you shut the door of the Kingdom of Heaven in people's faces. You won't go in yourselves, and you don't let others enter either. What sorrow awaits you teachers of religious law and you Pharisees. Hypocrites! For you cross land and sea to make one convert, and then you turn that person into twice the child of hell you yourselves are! . . . What sorrow awaits you teachers of religious law and you Pharisees. Hypocrites! For you are careful to tithe even the tiniest income from your herb gardens, but you ignore the more important aspects of the law—justice, mercy, and faith. You should tithe, yes, but do not neglect the more important things. Blind guides! You strain your water so you won't accidentally swallow a gnat, but you swallow a camel! What sorrow awaits you teachers of religious law and you Pharisees. Hypocrites! For you are so careful to clean the outside of the cup and the dish, but inside you are filthy—full of greed and self-indulgence! You blind Pharisee! First wash the inside of the cup and the dish, and then the outside will become clean, too. What sorrow awaits you teachers of religious law and you Pharisees. Hypocrites! For you are like whitewashed tombs—beautiful on the outside but filled on the inside with dead people's bones and all sorts of impurity. Outwardly you look like righteous people, but inwardly your hearts are filled with hypocrisy and lawlessness. What sorrow awaits you teachers of religious law and you Pharisees. Hypocrites! For you build tombs for the prophets your ancestors killed, and you decorate the monuments of the godly people your ancestors destroyed. (Matthew 23:13–15, 23–29 NLT).

Jesus called this particular group of religious leaders a "brood of vipers" (see Matthew 12:34; 23:33). Their forefathers were killers, and they were too. They carried lethal venom. Jesus was not only talking about their words or teachings; he was foreshadowing his own gruesome crucifixion.

Several species of vipers still inhabit the region in which Jesus lived. They are primarily nocturnal animals. They hunt under the cover of darkness and often hide under a thin covering of sand. When their prey is in range, they strike and inject toxic venom into the bloodstream. It causes internal bleeding, tissue damage, and death, even to humans. What a potent image to attach to a religious hypocrite!

Jesus' accusations against the group centered on their duplicity. They acted one way on the outside, but inside they were different. They were concerned about making a good appearance, but the state of their hearts was a mess. They followed the rules, but they lacked love. They were religious, but they were not godly. Do these accusations sound familiar? Have you ever met someone you thought was just in it for the applause of others? Hypocrites are controlling and self-concerned. They abuse their authority and mislead others. They confuse God's love with legalism. Jesus asks them, "How will you escape the judgment of hell?"

It sounds like Jesus is much more upset about hypocrisy than most of the people I know. His first and greatest judgment was that those leaders failed to recognize and love him. The way they treated Jesus was the main concern. Instead of welcoming him as Lord, they conspired toward his demise. Instead of giving him their lives, they tried to trip him up with trick questions. When the truth came out, it revealed their hearts were resistant to Jesus. The second key problem was that they were self-centered. Instead of loving their neighbors as themselves, they just loved themselves. These people wore the decorative garments of religious professors. They bathed in the awe of the commoners. They appeared to have it together, but their hearts were far from God.

who holds the gavel

Hypocrites don't represent God. God does not want people to make a flamboyant religious show and then live only for themselves. Jesus severely condemned this kind of behavior. Jesus seemed more bothered by religious hypocrites than by nonreligious sinners who committed adultery, theft, or even murder. God wants a person whose heart is right and whose actions follow.

Jesus is a good judge of hypocrites; we are not. He sees clearly into their motivations. Only he can accurately assess their hearts and hand out judgments. When we try to do this, we are not only inadequate, but also disobedient. "Do not judge [others], or you too will be judged," Jesus said (Matthew 7:1). Why are we so quick to accuse people of being hypocritical? When we do this, we often escalate the stakes by throwing out God and the whole Christian church because of the foul actions of one or two people. If this issue of hypocrites really is a barrier, let's break through it. This first requires a fresh look at the players involved.

the first players: me, myself, and eye

"Why worry about a speck in your friend's eye when you have a log in your own?" (Matthew 7:3 NLT).

A friend once accused me of being immature, rude, and overbearing. I had made an unintentional mistake, and he pounced on it. His tone was condescending and his words were cutting. I immediately felt that everything he was saying to me was true about him. He was being immature, rude, and overbearing. Talk about hypocritical. So what did I do? I listened. I went home and reflected on his words. I examined my actions and motivations carefully. I talked it over with a few trusted friends, and I talked it over with God. After several days, my anger subsided and my thoughts became clear. Some of the accusations he hurled at me I took as constructive criticism and learned from them. The rest I threw in the garbage can of the forgotten and forgiven past. Then, having spent several days examining myself, I addressed this conflict with my friend.

I cannot tell you how many times I have accused another person of something that I was guilty of myself. The reason I cannot tell you is because I don't know. We often point the finger at another's fault when we should be grasping for a mirror instead. When our eyes are fixed on another person's blemish, we have no time to address our own. Sometimes we even recognize our own shortcomings and instead of owning up to them, we project them onto another person.

People will disappoint you. No doubt about that. Even Christians will do it sometimes. If you have a knack for finding faults, your radar will always be blinking red. The reality is that hypocrites will always have a dynamic effect on you. They will cause you to grow or go. It's your choice. But be careful, because if you make a pattern of jumping ship every time someone on the crew is mean to you, you will have a long and lonely swim. What would that pattern look like if it bled over into your marriage? Your job? Your schoolwork? Your kids and grandkids? What about yourself? Would you give up on yourself the first time you acted like a hypocrite?

Perhaps the easiest way to stop being hypocrites is to stop pretending to be good Christians. We can fool ourselves into thinking that if we don't identify ourselves with God and the church then we won't fail to meet anyone's expectations. This might be a good strategy if our goals were to set the bar low and never disappoint anyone. But not being hypocritical is more daring than that. We want to take Jesus up on his promise. If he is the way, the truth, and the life, and everything else is a dead end, the hideout technique doesn't cut it. Without him we are lost and longing for more.

The first step in breaking through the barrier of hypocrisy is shifting focus. We must start by examining our own lives. Is there anything in your life that you preach but don't practice?

the other players

weeds and wheat

This past spring I planted a garden for the first time in my life. It was our anniversary, and my wife and I spent half the day outside digging in the dirt. I removed the top layer of grass. Then I tilled the ground with a shovel using the double-dig method. Esther mixed the dirt with a pitchfork after I dug it up. Then we added compost. Finally, we planted the seeds.

Since this was my first garden, I didn't know if we planted the seeds well. When they sprouted and started growing into plants, I quickly realized that some of the plants were too close together, and some of the sprouts were invasive weeds. They would soon be in competition for the soil and space and would have to be removed.

Jesus told a story about planting seeds. A man planted good wheat seeds in the ground, but at night his enemy came and planted weed seeds in the same plot. The wheat and weeds grew together, but the farmer waited until the harvest to separate them. The weeds went to the burn pile, and the wheat went to

the barn. (See Matthew 13:24–30, 36–43.) Based on this narrative, we realize that the true church is not necessarily the
pew church. In other words, some people who attend local
churches may not be following Christ at all. The wheat and
the weeds grow together. Just because they are in the same
place doesn't mean they are the same plant.

A Christian produces crops like love, joy, peace, patience,
kindness, goodness, faithfulness, gentleness, and self-control
(Galatians 5:22–23). The reason some people are not showing
the crops of a Christian is because they aren't Christians. They
might hang out in the right places with the right people. They
might read the Bible or pray. They might be moral. But just as
wearing a basketball jersey doesn't make you an athlete, going
to church doesn't make you a Christian.

Are there hypocrites in the church? Sure. Some may even
be in danger of the fires of hell, to use the words of Jesus.
(We'll talk about heaven, hell, and judgment in chapter 8.)
They are religious and concerned with outward appearance,
but they haven't had a heart change or a saving relationship
with Jesus. I am more concerned for them than I am angry.
God can do the separating and the judging. Not me. I want to
make sure I am wheat and try to help weeds become wheat.

doctors and sick people

One sign of a healthy church is that it has some sick people.
Worship services are not pep rallies for perfect people. Jesus
intentionally spent time with those who were spiritually ill. He

didn't want to hang around religious people who thought they were already good enough and had it all together. Why? Because his mission was to bring healing and life. Those who know they're sick also know they need to get well. But those who are blind to their spiritual diseases won't accept a cure. So your church should be admitting patients with serious life problems. The goal of a doctor, and likewise that of a hospital, is to make the patient well. So while the church is never a holding pen for dysfunction, it is a community in the process of healthy transformation. We are all growing.

What happens if you catch someone on a bad day? He or she may yell at you out of spiritual illness instead of treating you with kindness. Is there room for tempers, gossip, and mistakes in the church? Sure. These are symptoms of a deeper disease called sin. Even those who follow Jesus and have been forgiven still have bouts with sin sometimes. There's room for imperfections only because there's room for imperfect people. But God doesn't accept our sins. He wants us completely cured. Sometimes this takes a very long time. If God has room for people in progress, shouldn't we?

God

If you have been personally hurt by a hypocrite, know that God did not do it. His intention toward you is love. He wants what is best for you, and he'll go to any lengths to rescue you. He even responded to the religious leaders in Matthew by ultimately showing them the greatest act of love possible—dying for them . . . and for you. When we leave it up to God to judge others, we can take a rest from it ourselves. And without the burden of playing God, we are free to enjoy his love more fully. And the more fully we are drenched in his love, the more we will love others. The more we love others, the more we live up to who we are meant to be. People will see that kind of love and know it's strange. It almost seems supernatural. It is; it comes from God.

handling hypocrites

There is a difference between a hypocrite (someone who pretends to be perfect on the outside but whose inner life is wicked) and a growing Christian (who strives to live a life of love and still makes mistakes). Only God can change hearts. We can pray for those who appear to be living examples of hypocrisy. God will certainly judge their lives as he will judge ours. I would not follow a Christian leader who I felt was hypocritical. Nor would I want anyone to follow me unless they trusted my character. There are some people who are not trustworthy and some leaders who should not be followed. The most well-known Christian leaders are often the ones who get the biggest publicity when they mess up. Their failures tend to black mark the entire name of Christians. While their breach of integrity might be a good reason to stop financially supporting their ministries or to stop entrusting them with your loved ones, it is not a good excuse to abandon the church and give up on following Jesus. Instead of fleeing, Jesus wants us to face hurts and wrongs head on. Here's how.

abuse of authority

People have high expectations of Christian public figures because of their positions. When they make mistakes or abuse their authority, it's good to acknowledge that they were acting inconsistently with what God wanted for them. He—not us— will bring justice for their wrongs. Instead, we can pray for them and those they have hurt. And then we should learn from their failures and not repeat them.

personal hurts

To the person who gossiped behind your back, to the old lady who sneered at you, to the preacher who lost his temper— it's time to address the hurt face-to-face. If there are those within the church who emotionally hurt you, it is your responsibility to talk with them. Bring it up; set up a meeting. Tell them how they made you feel and ask if that's what they intended. It's easy to say a thousand words about the problem to someone else, but it's very hard to say ten words to the person who caused it. Yet that is exactly what we must do. It's the only way toward reconciliation. And reconciliation is God's goal. He wants restored relationships within his family. Forgiveness and love can happen when face-to-face conversations occur. It takes more courage to engage than to refrain.

If the conflict you have with someone is not important enough to address in person, then forgive it, forget it, and drop it. Don't bring it up again, and don't hold a grudge. If you're not willing to do this, then it's time to talk with the person. If you do talk but nothing is resolved, at least you have made an honest effort. Keep praying and leave room for God's Spirit to work.

be the change

A hypocrite may cause you to doubt yourself. If other Christians can't live rightly, what makes you think you can? Such thinking calls into question whether God can truly change a person's life or if it's all a sham. After putting our trust in one person after another and finding continual disappointment, we become jaded. Our ability to trust deteriorates. When we begin to doubt God, we also cast a shadow onto ourselves. Hope fades, and the idea of living like Jesus becomes a taunting delusion.

Do you know what Jesus said about the narrow road? It's narrow. Few find it. Following Jesus is rare, but it's not impossible. Just because someone else side-trailed onto the broad path doesn't mean you have to. I refuse to fall away because of someone else's mistakes. Life is too important. Besides, maybe God will touch the hypocrite's heart and he or she will find forgiveness. Who knows? God might even use you to help that happen.

For every spotlighted Christian who lives a double life, there are hundreds of unsung heroes who quietly love others every day. Their step-by-step journey of authenticity does not show up on the news. People don't rally around them and cry, "The church is full of saints! I'm going to join." They are not in it for the show; they are in it for the Lord. These people did not turn back at their first brush with hypocrisy. Their trust was never fully in people anyway; it is in God. That is why they can consistently love others.

Are you going to let a hypocrite be the fence between you and Jesus? Or will you allow God to demonstrate through you what the Christian life of love really looks like? Some people say they don't believe in God or go to church because there are so many hypocrites. Maybe. But I bet that reason is often a veil for something deeper. Something like pain and suffering, which we'll discuss in the next chapter.

questions for reflection

What experiences have you had with hypocrites?

How have they affected your faith?

questions for action

If you have acted like a hypocrite and hurt someone, how can you go back to the person and make it right?

Based on your negative experiences with hypocrites, make a positive motivation list for yourself in the future.

Out of suffering
have emerged the
strongest souls; the most
massive characters are
seared with scars.

—Kahlil Gibran

5

pain and suffering

intruder

Have you ever seen a child wipe out? Yesterday I watched a three-year-old playing next to her mother. Suddenly she slipped and fell on her back. The adults paused. Little Brittney looked up at Mommy. There was a moment of silence. You could almost read her thoughts: "What happened? Ouch! That hurt. The grown-ups look like something's wrong. Maybe I should cry!"

At first she was surprised. Brittney was having fun. Then, all of a sudden, pain interrupted. It didn't fit. It wasn't welcome. Puzzlement preceded tears. Why is pain here on such a happy day? Does it really have the right to barge in any time I make a slip-up? Despite the fact that it is not welcome, pain remains. The fall hurts. And Brittney wails.

Even more somber than her shock at the pain was the look she gave her mother. Lying flat on the ground, she shot an expressive glance upward, as if to say, "Mommy, I can't believe you let me fall! Why didn't you stop this? How could you?" The older we get, the harder we fall. If only adult wounds were limited to scraped knees or bloody lips. If only we could cry a minute, get a hug, and keep playing. But the damage is much more pervasive than that. My friend Cameron falls in love. He's convinced she's the one he's going to marry, the one God made just for him. He tangles up his spiritual life with his romantic pursuits. Then she breaks his heart. Another friend, Laura, is married for a few short years and discovers her husband has been habitually unfaithful. Next comes a painful divorce. Another friend, Jack, a teenager, ends his life at the end of a shotgun barrel. A girl I know cuts herself regularly when she's upset. Another forces herself to vomit. Another is on anti-depressants. A guy who suffered childhood abuse now unleashes his rage on others. A child is born with a crippling illness. A spouse dies too young.

You know these people too, by different names. You probably have some scars yourself. Maybe they're not even scars yet, maybe they're still seeping, open lacerations. You might hide them from the public eye with layers of clothing. But they bleed through your coverings and stain your relationships. If you have somehow managed to go through life relatively unscathed, don't get cocky and take off your seatbelt. There is likely to be turbulence ahead.

the voyage of life

I can still vividly recall staring at those huge paintings for the first time. They whispered untranslatable wisdom to my soul. I didn't grasp their full meaning back then, but I knew that I must remember them. I blazed those images into my mind and hid them away. I kept them in a sacred place so I could visit them during important moments of life. In the 1840s, Thomas Cole painted a series of four works called *The Voyage of Life*.[1] I first experienced them at the Indianapolis Art Museum right before I entered the third painting in my own life.

The first painting is called *Childhood*. It portrays a newborn baby on a small boat. He is emerging from a cave into a lush wilderness landscape. The boat, an ornately crafted vessel hardly bigger than a canoe, is steered by a radiant angel. Flowers are in bloom on the banks of the river. The sun is rising. The mountains are watching in awe at this new birth.

In the second painting, entitled *Youth*, the baby has grown up. He has taken the rudder in hand as the angel waves from the river's edge. The youth looks to the sky, to a mirage of a glorious castle floating above the distant mountains. The surrounding flora is taller now, and off in the horizon is a pink hue—the color of hopes and dreams.

The third piece is called *Manhood*. The scenery has changed. The quiet river has turned into treacherous rapids riddled with jagged rocks. The only vegetation is a gnarled tree gripping onto the rocks. Dark clouds swirl in the sky, and in them are the faces of evil tormenters hovering above the man in the boat. The man's hands are no longer steering the rudder. They are clasped in prayer. His thick beard and wind-blown hair surround a fearful expression. In the top corner, behind the boat, a light breaks through the clouds and the angel is barely visible.

I'll get to the fourth painting later.

Why are these paintings so important? Because they describe life. Childhood and youth are a time of dreaming. A magical passage through a golden wilderness. Even people who have had a traumatic childhood would still confess that it had a sort of rosy innocence to it. We confidently set off to pursue mansions in the sky. What could go wrong? The truth is, lots of things go wrong. The smooth sailing turns into dangerous waters. We may go weeks or months without a ray of hope. We might not be able to see the angel. Our rudder could break, and we may find ourselves cascading down challenges of life that we did not foresee in our youth.

Life hurts. At first the pain comes as a surprise. We wonder why this is happening to us. Pain is like a rude neighbor who crashes our party. We wish we could simply just tell him to leave. But it doesn't work. After the shock wears off, and the pain sets in, we often have another reaction. We look up to the sky and say, "Why, God? How could you let this happen to me? What have I done to deserve this?"

Here is where the road diverges. At the presence of pain and suffering in their lives, many people choose a broad and well-traveled way that does not lead to full life. This road may wind around, but it will eventually lead to self-pity, defeat, despair, and death. But we have a choice. We can walk the narrow road, the one that leads to life. It may be rare and elusive. It might be harder to find. But it's worth searching for, because life is at stake. Jesus is on that road. He is that road, and he wants to give us life.

head first

Pain and suffering affect our bodies, but the real threat is to our hearts. We can endure physical distress when there is hope. But when the presence of suffering in our lives erodes our trust in God, we quickly lose heart. And if we lose heart, we are as good as dead already.

Our hearts are at stake, but first let's address the head. We will look at some possible ways to understand pain and suffering. If we can think about this topic in the right way, our thoughts will form good beliefs. And when we believe the truth with all our hearts, we can persevere through the trials because we have hope.

So what is true? Does God bring tragedy into our lives?

It's important to realize that pain is not suffering. Pain itself is a gift. It is an unavoidable warning system for our bodies. Pain actually protects us. When we get splinters in our fingers, pain sends us a message telling us to get them out of there. When we touch hot stoves, pain tells us to move our hands. In a perfect world, pain would always prevent greater harm to our bodies. In our world, however, sometimes pain itself seems to be the greater harm. Sometimes the degree of pain seems unjustified.

Suffering is even worse. Its assault doesn't stop with our bodies. Sometimes it warns us to change; other times it is the result of things we cannot change. Suffering can destroy our morale or bring agony to our spirits. It is pain without purpose. And it lingers. Suffering is always unwelcome. We wonder why it was allowed to crash in. Suffering causes us to turn to God. We either look to him for comfort, or we ask the age-old question: Why? Many have abandoned their faith during the fires of suffering not only because of the torment, but because they cannot reconcile it with their personal view of God. Essentially, the conflict lies in this question: "If God is both all-loving and all-powerful, why is there evil and suffering in the world?"

Without an answer, it's hard to hope in God or pray for relief. So let's take a look at six possible ways to answer that question.

there is no God

This is atheism. Some atheists cite science or philosophy as the reason for their unbelief. Others have more personal reasons. Suffering in the world is not compatible with their understanding of God, so they face a crisis. One way to solve it is to remove God from the equation. Because there is evil and suffering in the world, they conclude there is no higher power. They give up on God. Though this decision is rational, it is also personal and painful. They get wounded and walk away, or they never believe in God in the first place. Their rallying cry is, "There is no God, and I hate him."

To give up on God is a tragic leap of faith. But it does seem to eliminate the tension of the suffering question. Without God to blame, suffering simply just is. It reduces the world to matter without meaning. It says pain simply exists in the world. Remedy it if you can; otherwise deal with it. You're on your own.

let's fix it ourselves

This response can be seen in extreme forms of humanism, social activism, or liberalism. People in this group may believe in God, but they put their faith in humanity. Evil is seen as the illegitimate child of ignorance. If only people were more educated, more aware, and better equipped, they would make the right decisions. This perspective sees humanity as primarily good and the world as a realm of infinite potential for improvement. This group doesn't waste much time blaming God for the pain and suffering in the world, nor do they really believe he can do much to help. They believe that the responsibility for righting the situation rests on the shoulders of every person. They march forward armed with technology, reason, information, and human kindness. Their rallying cry is, "We can change the world!"

this is the best possible world

This group believes that God is in charge and he knows what he's doing. They may not like pain and suffering, but they shouldn't question God's ways. Everything that happens is for a reason, and they should accept it. This world is the best God could do. They may not understand some things, but their job is to trust him. It was God's will that his child died at age six. It was God's will that her grandmother got cancer. Yes, it hurts, but this group believes you should just have faith. This perspective allows people to maintain faith in God, but with a resignation toward the more insufferable aspects of reality. Their rallying cry is, "God knows best."

God is punishing us

When bad things happen, some people look for divine motivations. They think God must be punishing them for their sins. They imagine that if God is in charge of the world and a tsunami ravages a coastal city, then God must have caused it and he must have a good reason. People in this group sometimes make arguments from the Old Testament, saying that God brought destruction to the Israelites because of their unbelief. Why wouldn't he do it again? Their rallying cry is, "God makes bad stuff happen to bad people for a good reason."

God doesn't care

This group might believe that there is a God but that he is not personally interested in their lives. They abandon the belief in God's loving nature toward humanity. They are practical atheists. If God is there but doesn't care, then they are on their own again. No use in praying. No use in hoping for heavenly help. God is not interested in their plight. Their rallying cry is, "If there is a God, he is the devil."

God cares but can't help

This perspective likens God to an endearing old grandfather. He cares about his grandchildren. He sees them walking in front of a bus. He tries to rush over to save them. But alas, he's too slow. He can't prevent the tragedy taking place before his eyes. This theory gives up on the omnipotence of God. Then what? They are left with warm hearts because God cares about them. But he's still not able to help them. They are on their own again. Their rallying cry is, "God's heart is strong, but his helping hand is weak."

There are certainly other ways to deal with the God-and-suffering question besides the ones mentioned here, and there are various ways to express the six addressed. But these perspectives give us a general map of the territory we're venturing through. It is rugged terrain, the kind of wilderness where many are lost forever or eaten by wild animals. I'm not being overdramatic either. When people find themselves in the valley of the shadow of death, many make it their final resting place. They let pain snuff out their faith. If their minds can find no answers and their hearts can find no hope, suffering can cripple their souls.

not good enough

These six perspectives are all attempts to resolve an ancient question, but I am not satisfied with any of them. They are all inadequate. Here's why.

atheism leads to despair

Neither science nor philosophy has convinced me that there is no God. But even if I did come to believe this, the consequences would be unthinkable. If God doesn't exist, life is meaningless. We can ascribe meaning and value to life, but they will be unfounded because there are no standards of measurement other than personal opinion or corporate consensus. There is no purpose for which we were created because we are only the result of blind natural forces. There is no hope in life after death or life after jaded faith. There is no shot at lasting happiness. Even in despair, there is no meaning, because meaning necessitates a worthy desire or goal that was unattained. There would be no standard for morality or social justice. No transcendent element to love, romance, courage, ecstasy, sacrifice, or achievement. All human emotions and experiences would be reduced to various chemical or biological functions. Cause and effect. No meaning. No purpose. No cosmic figure to love us, right the wrongs of history, or help us face death.

I have stood on the edge of this cliff and peered down into its abyss. It is a scary black hole. The thought of jumping off the solid ground on which I stood and plummeting into the darkness of atheism made me shudder. I couldn't do it. I couldn't bring myself to accept that all we are is material creatures surviving in a material world that has absolutely no point. The Bible begins with a different assumption, a more hopeful one. The opening sentence introduces God. It doesn't explain him or argue for why he exists. It simply introduces him. We don't weave him into our reality; it is he who made reality from scratch. "In the beginning God created the heavens and the earth" (Genesis 1:1). Anyone can believe that God doesn't exist. But I wouldn't want to. While it might ease the God-and-suffering crisis, it washes away all that is valuable in the process.

we can't fix it ourselves

A friend of mine served in the Peace Corps in the Middle East for several years. This guy has a huge heart. He has a passion to work for peace and justice, and he has a glowing affinity for Arabic culture. The Peace Corps was a good match for him. When he completed his service time, we talked about burnout. He explained that many people enter the Peace Corps with high expectations. They believe they can make a difference. By the end, many are humbled by the vastness of the need and their limited ability to help.

I admire and respect anyone who works to improve the world. I want to make a difference too! I believe we can change the world, but not all by ourselves. The problem with this view is misdiagnosis. If people only need resources and education, our job description would be to supply and teach. However, knowing what's right doesn't mean doing what's right. A change of heart is needed, and divine aid is required. Human efforts and energies alone will not succeed in addressing the pain and suffering in the world. Human efforts partnering with God's infinite love and resources can make a lasting difference. I have felt the burnout of trying to help in a developing nation. I couldn't sustain a faith that was solely in humanity. I had to root my faith in God, and then I could work from a position of strength.

"Unless the LORD builds a house, the work of the builders is wasted. Unless the LORD protects a city, guarding it with sentries will do no good. It is useless for you to work so hard from early morning until late at night, anxiously working for food to eat; for God gives rest to his loved ones" (Psalm 127:1–2 NLT).

God works for our good

God is not in heaven waiting to kill the mother and newborn during birth so he can have another couple of "angels in his choir." He doesn't cause airplanes to crash or children to get leukemia. It bothers me when someone blames tragedy and suffering on God's will. He does not arbitrarily destroy us and then tell us to trust in his goodness. This would lead to a kind of spiritual schizophrenia. How could we be expected to love a God who brings pain, suffering, and death to us? Is it enough to say that he has a bigger perspective and it will all work out for the best? No. This implies that we have no moral compass whatsoever. If what we know as the worst kind of evil is really God's good plan, then we are entirely unstable and God is malicious.

God is a mystery. We cannot know all of his ways. He does, however, work out even the worst situations for our good. But that does not mean he steals from us or kills us for fun. It doesn't mean we should expect the unpredictable at the hand of God—a loving touch or a crushing blow. Jesus pointed to a different culprit as the enemy of humanity: "The thief comes only to steal and kill and destroy; I have come that [people] may have life, and have it to the full" (John 10:10).

Later we will discuss how God can bring good out of evil and how he uses pain and suffering to shape us. But it should not be assumed that the bad things in our lives are somehow God's will. Scripture gives us numerous examples to the contrary. In John 11:35, "Jesus wept" over the death of his friend Lazarus. He gave no indication that this death was God's doing. Instead, he brought Lazarus back to life. Later, before he was crucified, Jesus told his disciples to expect hard times: "In this world you will have trouble. But take heart! I have overcome the world" (John 16:33). Jesus did not say, "Take heart! It is God who gives you trouble. Just trust in him. It'll be OK." Instead, he talked about a battle between this world and God's kingdom.

It would be sad if we were already living in the best possible world. In the beginning, the Bible gives us a picture of a garden that was free of pain and suffering. And in the end, it gives us a vision of a new earth where there are no tears. God is working in this world—the one that he created—to redeem us and eventually overthrow the forces responsible for pain and suffering.

we must be cautious in proclaiming God's judgment on anyone
There are cases in the Bible where God punished a person or group for their sin. He punished Cain for killing his brother Abel (see Genesis 4:10–13). The kingdom of Israel was conquered by Assyria in 722 B.C. because of their rebellion against God (see Amos 2:6–8). The kingdom of Judah was conquered by Babylon in 586 B.C. for the same reason (see Micah 2:1–5). Ananias and Sapphira dropped dead after lying about their money (see Acts 5:1–11). These stories and others show us that God punishes sin. Other places in Scripture are even more direct about the divine judgment each of us will face at the end of our lives. However, this does not give us a license to interpret bad things as God's punishment on others. God gave repeated warnings to Israel and Judah before he destroyed them. He wanted them to repent. The prophetic books of Amos, Hosea, Joel, Isaiah, Micah, Zephaniah, Jeremiah, Habakkuk, and Lamentations are devoted to the message and warnings of God's impending punishment on the nations. God made it clear what he was doing.

Jesus encountered the "God is punishing us" perspective from his own disciples. They met a man who was blind from birth. And the disciples asked, "Who sinned, this man or his parents, that he was born blind?" They assumed that the suffering in his life was a punishment for sin. What did Jesus say? "Neither" (John 9:2–3). The man's blindness wasn't a punishment for sin. We should not normally presume to interpret other people's pain and suffering as divine judgment.

God cares for us

If we were talking about an arbitrary deity we neither know nor relate to, we might conclude that he is unconcerned with our situations. But if we are talking about the God who reveals himself to the world and made his biggest statement in Jesus Christ, then we cannot maintain a conviction that he doesn't care about us. Jesus, who suffered a painful death, taught his disciples that God cared for each of them intimately. He said that "the very hairs of your head are all numbered" (Luke 12:7). His suffering did not lead him to conclude God didn't care. Neither did Paul's pain cause him to doubt God's love. Paul was tortured, ridiculed, locked away, lost at sea, and eventually executed for his life of devotion to Jesus. Yet he frequently wrote to his Christian friends about God's "great love for us" (Ephesians 2:4).

God is matchless

To understand the word *matchless*, think of wrestling. No one can pin God. He's too big and strong. He's too fierce. He's better than all his opponents because he created them. No rival has a fighting chance at winning. So to say that God has a warm heart but a weak arm is a misrepresentation. If he created the universe, surely he cannot be helpless when it comes to the problem of suffering.

But if there is a God who loves us and has the power to help, the question remains: Why doesn't he? So far all we've done is discuss why the first six explanations are inadequate. Now let's look at the problem from a different perspective. There is a war, and we are in the midst of battle.

war and freedom

God gave us life. He's a proud father who adores his kids. He wants the best for us. And what exactly is the best for us? He is. God wants a relationship with us, but he won't force us into it. He built into us a freedom factor. We can choose whom we love and how we live. And humanity has been making wrong choices from the beginning. We have chosen a friendship with God's enemies and made ourselves enemies of his love. The Bible traces much of our pain and suffering back to this freedom.

We are players in an ongoing cosmic war. There's no doubt God will win this war when the time is right. It's our fate that is yet to be decided. Jesus is trying to lead us on the narrow path to life. The Evil One is trying to entice us off of it. This brings us to the why of suffering.

There are many possible causes for suffering. We may not like any of them, but none of them take us beyond God's care and power. Some of our suffering is a result of the Devil and his forces working against us. He is the thief that comes to steal our joy, kill our bodies, and destroy our souls. Some of our suffering is a result of our own choices. Other times God could be punishing or disciplining us. And there are some times in which suffering simply cannot be explained. In our relationships with God who is mysterious, we can coexist with the inexplicable without surrendering our faith.

This talk of war and freedom still brings more questions: Why would God give us freedom if he knew it could cause such disaster? What about natural disasters like earthquakes and tornados? Why do innocent people sometimes suffer for other people's mistakes?

job's answer

Remember Job? No one has asked the question, "Why, God?" with as much force as Job. He suffered severely. And the story clearly depicts Job as innocent. So why do the innocent suffer? The book of Job tells us that he did not suffer because of his own sins or the sins of someone in his family. He did not suffer because God was punishing him. He did not suffer because God didn't exist, didn't care, or couldn't help. God was aware and in charge the whole time. So why did Job suffer?

Job was in so much pain that he wished he had never been born. He was angry at God. He accused God of being unfair. He wanted answers, just like we want answers. We want something rational to make sense of our suffering. We want to know why. Even if we recognize that our difficulties stem from the forces of evil, our own mistakes, or God's punishment, it's not enough. We still wonder why this evil and its pain exist in the first place. Why does God allow it? Why us?

Job received an answer to his questions. God was not silent forever.

The book of Job can be broken into three different sections. The first two chapters are a description of Job's life and the tragedies that befell him. Chapters 3–37 contain arguments and conversations between Job and his friends. In chapters 38–42, God finally spoke with Job. That's thirty-seven chapters of suffering and wondering before God made an appearance. After all that waiting, what did God say?

God answered Job's question with a question: "Who is this that darkens my counsel with words without knowledge? Brace yourself like a man; I will question you, and you shall answer me. Where were you when I laid the earth's foundation?" (Job 38:2–4). God's questions revealed Job's smallness. Job wasn't around when God made the earth and created the animals. He was in no position to even comprehend how God runs the world. After a forceful display of interrogation, God finished his speech and Job responded: "Surely I spoke of things I did not understand, things too wonderful for me to know. . . . My ears had heard of you but now my eyes have seen you" (Job 42:3, 5).

God's presence was the answer. He offered no logical arguments, no sensible appeals or apologies. He just showed up, and Job had a change of heart. Job didn't get a solid answer on the why question. That remained a mystery. But his suffering was put into perspective. He encountered the greatness of God and knew that the proper response was faith. And in Job's story, God's goodness had the final word.

Our pain will probably never fully make sense. It is always an unwelcome intruder. It is good to ask God why. He may not give us a satisfactory explanation, but if we turn to him, he will be with us. His presence is our answer. We can choose to focus on unanswered questions, or we can focus on our responses. Those who are fixated on the why often grow bitter and angry. Those who say, "What can I do?" become pioneers to others who travel in the land of suffering.

what can i do?

feel the pain

Grieve. Cry. Yell. Let it out. Just because you follow Jesus doesn't make you immune to pain. Sometimes it makes you more sensitive to it. The first step in dealing with pain and suffering is to acknowledge what is really happening and how you feel. If something bad happens, it's OK to be sad. It's good to cry over the loss of a friend. God does not want us to put on a cheap, happy face in the midst of great suffering. The Psalms give some poignant expressions of grief. The fact that these kinds of songs were included in the Bible validates their place in the human experience.

Take a look at Psalms 5–6, 13, 22, 38, 42, 54–64, 69, 74, 77, 102, 137, 140, and 143. Read, sing, or scream them to God. Tell him how you're feeling. Be brutally honest. Hit hard. He can handle it. He's not scared of how you're feeling.

O LORD, God of my salvation, I cry out to you by day. I come to you at night. Now hear my prayer; listen to my cry. For my life is full of troubles, and death draws near. I am as good as dead, like a strong man with no strength left. They have left me among the dead, and I lie like a corpse in a grave. I am forgotten, cut off from your care. You have thrown me into the lowest pit, into the darkest depths. Your anger weighs me down; with wave after wave you have engulfed me. You have driven my friends away by making me repulsive to them. I am in a trap with no way of escape. My eyes are blinded by my tears. Each day I beg for your help, O LORD; I lift my hands to you for mercy. Are your wonderful deeds of any use to the dead? Do the dead rise up and praise you? Can those in the grave declare your unfailing love? Can they proclaim your faithfulness in the place of destruction? Can the darkness speak of your wonderful deeds? Can anyone in the land of forgetfulness talk about your righteousness? O LORD, I cry out to you. I will keep on pleading day by day. O LORD, why do you reject me? Why do you turn your face from me? I have been sick and close to death since my youth. I stand helpless and desperate before your terrors. Your fierce anger has overwhelmed me. Your terrors have paralyzed me. They swirl around me like floodwaters all day long. They have engulfed me completely. You have taken away my companions and loved ones. Darkness is my closest friend. (Psalm 88 NLT)

let it make you stronger

Don't try to rush through the grieving process. Wrestle with God for awhile. If you do, you will be like the butterfly that has fought its way out of the cocoon. You will be strong and you will fly. If you skip the wrestling part, your wings will be unfit for the journey ahead. It is when we are broken and at the end of our strength that we are able to become who we are intended to be. God uses challenges in our lives to build us and make us more like him. James, the brother of Jesus, told us, "Consider it pure joy . . . whenever you face trials of many kinds, because you know that the testing of your faith develops perseverance. Perseverance must finish its work so that you may be mature and complete, not lacking anything" (James 1:2–4).

God wants us to be happy, but not from a cheap thrill ride. He wants to forge us into mature people who have weathered life's storms and grown stronger. He wants us to become like Jesus, and this takes time. We may not be able to see the good things God is doing through our hardships yet. But we can have hope that our suffering is not purposeless. God is using it for our growth.

cling to Jesus

Our greatest comfort is not in understanding suffering. It's not even in knowing that God is using it for good. The best help is knowing that Jesus is with us. His disciples fled when he was beaten and crucified. He died alone on the cross. But we do not suffer alone. Jesus will not abandon us. He is with us for every tear, gasp, and strained heartbeat. He is familiar with our pain. He, too, has suffered. But he did not lose heart. His agony was greater than ours will ever be, and he persevered. He grabbed onto the hope of what was to come and refused to let pain break his grip. That same fierce grip is now holding onto your hand, refusing to let go.

old age

Now for painting number four. It is entitled *Old Age*. The waters are calm and the boat is still. The scenery is dark. The world has faded into the background. Bright rays of light beckon the eye heavenward as the angel descends to the old man. His boat is broken and worn. His hair is gray and his clothes are tattered. His hands are no longer clasped, but reaching out toward the angel who has come to guide him home. Another angel waits in the distance to welcome the old traveler to the final destination in his voyage of life.

Suffering and death do not have to have the final word. There is life after that. When the clouds break and the pain fades, we will stand on weary legs to face a fresh sunrise. When our lives on the earth are used up, our bodies will be renewed. We will stand next to Jesus as those who have suffered with him like warriors. With his finger, he will wipe away the tears streaming down our weathered faces. The love in his smile will flood our hearts, and our pain will pass from memory.

Pain and suffering, regardless of their causes, can bring us closer to God. They can shape us like an athlete conditioned through hard training. They give God an opportunity to display his healing power or his gracious comfort. They are temporary travelers with us on this voyage of life. And one day we will wave farewell to them as we approach the land that lies beyond old age.

questions for reflection

Do you know anyone whose faith has been shipwrecked by pain and suffering? What happened? What have you suffered in your life? How did it affect you? How did you respond to the suffering?

question for action

What will you do this week to encourage a friend who is suffering?

note

1. *The Voyage of Life: Childhood*, The Collection: National Gallery of Art, accessed June 26, 2012, http://www.nga.gov/fcgi-bin/tinfo_f?object=52167.0&detail=none.

6

rationalism

growing tensions

Christians are often portrayed in movies as lunatics. Their job descriptions appear to be something like this:

- Monday: Stand on the street corner with a sign that says, THE END IS NEAR.
- Tuesday: Knock on the doors of people you don't know, and ask them where they'll go when they die.
- Wednesday: Carry your Bible around, and quote random verses to passersby.
- Thursday: Give a two-cent prefabricated answer to a friend in crisis who has a million-dollar problem.

- Friday: Listen to music that makes no sense to everyone else, and close your eyes and pretend it means something to you.

- Saturday: Do something really stupid, like bomb an abortion clinic.

- Sunday: Get dressed up, go to church, and praise God with that same strange music. And then tell other people how many doors you knocked on that week.

Most people realize that Christianity is not defined or even accurately represented by Hollywood. However, there is a real, more subtle perception that shapes society's view of Christians. Some people are bold enough to say it in public; many others quietly think it to themselves. In classrooms, in laboratories, and at the office, the thought ruminates—that to be a Christian means you cannot be a rational person, that no educated person could believe in Noah's ark, Jonah's whale, and heaven and hell. A growing number of people in our society believe that Christians are just plain ignorant. To them the movie stereotypes are not far from the truth.

Who has more credibility: your professor or pastor? The science teacher at a public high school or the Bible teacher at your local Sunday school? Society has embraced a system of thought that has dethroned religion and given the chair to science and reason. I have met many people who are caught in this tension. They grew up believing in Jesus and learned about the Bible as children. Many were even baptized. But as they encountered new thoughts and ideas in school, their confidence in their Bible training waned.

Students intuitively feel the conflict of worldviews. They may not be able to articulate it, but they know that their church and school aren't teaching the same thing. The professor and pastor can't both be right, can they? If math, science, and philosophy—the areas that are ruled by fact, logic, and proof—are pointing me one direction, how can I follow the Bible in another? These inconsistencies reach a boiling point, and many leave their faith. They conclude that being rational means they can't follow Jesus.

not a new tension

The apostle Paul wrote to a group of Christians in a very unchristian city. They, too, were making tough decisions about what to believe. He said:

The message of the cross is foolish to those who are headed for destruction! But we who are being saved know it is the very power of God. . . . So where does this leave the philosophers, the scholars, and the world's brilliant debaters? God has made the wisdom of this world look foolish. Since God in his wisdom saw to it that the world would never know him through human wisdom, he has used our foolish preaching to save those who believe. It is foolish to the Jews who ask for signs from heaven. And it is foolish to the Greeks, who seek

human wisdom. So when we preach that Christ was crucified, the Jews are offended and the Gentiles say it's all
nonsense. (1 Corinthians 1:18, 20–23 NLT)

Paul said the message about Jesus seemed like nonsense to
many people. His preaching did not ring true to those on the
broad path. They were already headed for destruction. He
spoke of two different groups: Jews and Greeks. The Jews
wanted to see miracles and displays of power. They expected
their Messiah to rule as a king, not die as a criminal. They didn't
see how Jesus was worth following. After all, he claimed to
be God and then got himself killed. The Greeks did not understand Jesus either. He did not fit into their logical ideals. How
could someone rise from the dead? This idea is absurd.
Besides, any legitimate god of the Greeks would not have chosen crucifixion. Though much is different today, there is still
a similar tension.

But Paul said there is more at work than reason and proof.
Following Jesus is not only a matter of evidence; it's an issue
of the heart. A person's spiritual condition shapes his or her
mental cognition. Paul claimed that God did not create the kind
of world where people could know everything simply by their
reason and experience. Instead, God made himself known to
everyone, even simple and uneducated people. It doesn't
require any special degree or license to discover the truth. Anyone can know God and the truth about the universe. The first
step is faith in a God who is beyond the parameters of human

reason and experience. It is faith in a God who makes the first move and reveals himself to us. It is faith that the mind of God is bigger than the minds of humanity.

And so we have found our tension, right at the very beginning. Regardless of what you believe, your first step is faith. Even strict rationalists or empiricists who conclude that there is no deity start with faith. They begin their intellectual journey with the belief that humans can only discover what is true through reason and experience. They have only one eye open in their search for truth, the natural eye. The material world and their encounters with it define reality for them. They have faith in their tools of logic and science, and they have decided from the start to eliminate any other tools. So their findings, evidence, data, and conclusions will not exceed the scope of the material world because their tools are limited to it.

For Christians the first step is different. We believe that the one-eye approach is insufficient. We think humans cannot discover truth simply by using the limited tools of their reason and experience. We believe these two tools aren't even functioning properly because of the poor spiritual condition we are in. They're like flashlights that shine only a little into the darkness but cannot illuminate the whole landscape. Where the rationalist has infinite confidence in human knowledge and capabilities, the Christian places only limited confidence there. More is required. Man is not the measure of all things. There is something bigger than us in the universe—someone who created us and knows more than we do. We can know this someone, and our greatest insights will come from him. He is reasonable and knowledgeable, and we can experience him firsthand. But he will not be chained and caged by our naturalistic tools. He is the teacher; we are the students.

To learn from him, we must open our other eye—the spiritual eye. This is the eye that allows us to get our heads into the heavens instead of trying to get the heavens into our heads. This vision begins with faith in God, confirmed through the mind and senses. It is a more humble view of ourselves. With both eyes wide open, we can see that humans don't know everything and our world is messed up. We can see that the universe is designed. We can feel the weight of our hearts, that they desire purpose and direction. We can sense the guiding voice of God. We can skillfully apply science and reason to learn about the world God created. And we don't need to have double vision. The spiritual eye does not contradict the natural eye. They work together and bring reality into clearer focus.

great minds

Though many people today believe Christians are illogical, this was not always true. Christian history is full of scholars and brilliant writers who used their God-given intellect to explain their faith to critics and skeptics. Here are brief biographies of some of these great thinkers.

justin martyr (A.D. 100–165)

Justin Martyr's works include *First Apology*, *Second Apology*, and *Dialogue with Trypho*. He studied Greek philosophy until he converted to Christianity. He said of his newfound faith in Jesus, "A fire was suddenly kindled in my soul. I fell in love with the prophets and these men who had loved Christ; I reflected on all their words and found that this philosophy alone was true and profitable. That is how and why I became a philosopher. And I wish that everyone felt the same way that I do."[1] Justin was eventually tried, convicted, and beheaded for his faith.

irenaeus (ca. A.D. 125–202)

Irenaeus's greatest surviving work is *Against Heresies*, which he wrote to defend the Christian faith against Gnostic heresies. "Error, indeed, is never set forth in its naked deformity, lest, being thus exposed, it should at once be detected. But it is craftily decked out in an attractive dress, so as, by its outward form, to make it appear to the inexperienced (ridiculous as the expression may seem) more true than the truth itself."[2]

tertullian (ca. A.D. 160–220)

Tertullian was raised in a Roman household and converted to Christianity around the end of the second century. He wrote dozens of books on the Christian life and its defense against other belief systems and accusations. Some of his works include *Apologeticum*, *Against Marcion*, and *Against Hermogones*. "For reason is a property of God's, since there is nothing which God, the creator of all things, has not foreseen, arranged and determined by reason; moreover, there is nothing He does not wish to be investigated and understood by reason."[3]

origen (ca. A.D. 185–253)

Origen studied Greek philosophy and taught the worldview of Christianity to intellectuals, converting many to faith. One of his primary works was *On First Principles*. "For whatever be the knowledge which we are able to obtain of God, either by perception or reflection, we must of necessity believe that He is by many degrees far better than what we perceive Him to be."[4]

athanasius (ca. A.D. 297–373)

Athanasius argued for proper doctrine, especially in regard to the nature of Jesus, as in his *On the Incarnation of the Word of God*. "The Self-revealing of the Word is in every dimension—above, in creation; below, in the Incarnation; in the depth, in Hades; in the breadth, throughout the world. All things have been filled with the knowledge of God."[5]

augustine (A.D. 354–430)

After studying Manichaeism, Neoplatonism, and other forms of academic philosophy, Augustine gave his life to Christ. He recorded his intellectual and spiritual journey in his book *Confessions*. He wrote more than a hundred books in his lifetime on topics ranging from morality, the existence of God, philosophy, spirituality, and others. "You [God] stir man to take pleasure in praising you, because you have made us for yourself, and our heart is restless until it rests in you."[6]

The people mentioned above are only a handful of early Christian intellectuals. For over a thousand years in Western civilization, most scholars, philosophers, professors, and scientists were Christians. They believed God existed, and they belonged to the church. They sought to understand through their reason and experience the orderly world God made. Among these intellectuals are Anselm of Canterbury, Peter Abelard, Nicolus Copernicus, and Thomas Aquinas. Reading their works is like trying to walk through four feet of mud—thick, slow, and deep. These guys were not idiots. For instance in *Summa Theologica*, Aquinas wrote about the existence of God, whether sacred doctrine is required beyond philosophy and science, whether God is the supreme good, whether God can be known by natural reason, and whether God is changeless. Here is an excerpt, just as an example:

Wisdom is called mobile by way of similitude, according as it diffuses its likeness even to the outermost of things; for nothing can exist which does not proceed from the divine wisdom by way of some kind of imitation, as from the first effective and formal principle; as also works of art proceed from the wisdom of the artist. And so in the same way, inasmuch as the similitude of the divine wisdom proceeds in degrees from the highest things, which participate more fully of its likeness, to the lowest things which participate of it in a lesser degree.[7]

And so on. Brainy stuff. So how did the Christian faith go from the normative ground of reason to the supposed baseless religion of idiots? Simply stated, the Enlightenment was the catalyst that sparked change.

reason rules the day

In 1517 Martin Luther nailed his Ninety-Five Theses to the door of the church at Wittenberg in Germany. The world of Christianity subsequently went through major reconstruction, during a time period now referred to as the Reformation. Leaders like Luther, Zwingli, and Calvin wanted to reform the church and correct some of its errors. This was not a quick and easy process, and it wasn't welcomed by those in power. But it did happen. Through arguments, councils, splits, and even executions, change occurred.

One major change was that a new group branched off and formed several churches. They were called the Protestants (a derogatory name given to them because they protested against the established church). They upheld the authority of the Bible and pulled out the rug of authority from under the religious establishment. The power began trickling down to all believers, who learned they could have a direct relationship with God and read the Bible for themselves (that is, if they could read and if they could find a copy of the Bible!).

Along with religious change, Europe was also experiencing social upheaval. The church and government had been intertwined for centuries. The fights over how to worship turned into wars. The Wars of Religion, centered in France from 1562–1598, destroyed a generation. These bloody battles between Catholics and Protestants and various political authorities cost the lives of thousands of soldiers. Then followed the Thirty Years' War, which decimated many European nations, and the English Civil War with its competing religious interests.

Amidst these political and religious debacles, people began to search for a better way to resolve their conflicts than warfare. If this is what Christianity is all about, wouldn't it be safer to be an atheist? Philosophers and statesmen began to replace the authority of the church with a more objective power—the mind. René Descartes whittled philosophy down to its starting point: human thought. He said we can doubt everything except the fact that we doubt. Based on the foundation of our rational reflection, he said, we can build what is real in the world. Later thinkers like John Locke and Immanuel Kant revised and expanded upon the cornerstone of reason and connected experience as its counterpart. Scientific proof and logical certainty began to define the world of "fact." Facts could be hypothesized, tested, verified, and certified. They could withstand public scrutiny. Appeals to logic and repeatable experience were seen as a more reliable ground for making decisions than an appeal to a God-given right to power. So while the Reformation dug up the root of tradition, the Enlightenment started gnawing at the root of revelation. With the advent of this new way of thinking about the world came changes in technology, science, religious tolerance, and the status of the individual. Humans had high hopes in themselves. They thought that through science and reason, any problem could be solved. Sometimes this took extreme forms, such as the Cult of Reason, formed by several radical revolutionaries during the French Revolution as a "replacement" for the Catholic Church. The leaders of this cult said there were no gods. They even advocated for congregational services toward the worship of reason.

religion sent to the corner

With the triumph of reason and science, religion became displaced. For centuries the church had enjoyed privileged political power, a claim to the fundamental truths of the world, and an attitude of reverence from the masses. Now Christianity was seen as the disruptive kid in the classroom. She did not play by the school rules. She did not recite or revere the new ideologies. So she was sent to the corner while the rest of the class marched ahead. The march went much further than the original Enlightenment thinkers intended. While philosophers like Descartes and Kant believed in God, their intellectual offspring used the Enlightenment tools to carve out an arena for fact and shove subjects like religion into the realm of personal and unverifiable beliefs.

After the Enlightenment, fact verified by logic or empirical experimentation mattered most. Fact shaped nations and formed laws. Fact determined what people understood as truth. These new modes of truth-seeking bludgeoned Christianity on the head, drove a spear through her side, and nailed her to a pole to be the social mockery of the intellectuals and philosophers. The core claims of Christianity have had to struggle against the assault of philosophical materialism dressed in the garb of modern science.

Some post-Enlightenment thinkers doubted a God they could not see or prove. They doubted miracles that were written in an ancient book. They didn't see how a man could walk on water or rise from the dead. So they began pruning away anything they thought was useless. Among the first things to go were miracles. Miracles are nonrepeatable and break the laws of nature. So from this point of view they must be classified as religious mythology, only included in the Bible to illustrate a spiritual lesson. Once the supernatural was ruled out, the claim was made that all that exists is the natural (material) world and that it runs by predictable laws that are ultimately knowable by human beings. There was no room for God in this closed world, except maybe as a being who created it all and then left the scene. Cutting out the supernatural meant that the miracles in the Bible were not historical, that the resurrection of Jesus didn't happen, and that he was not the Son of God he claimed to be. What was left?

Enlightenment thought reduced religion to moral teachings, behavior training, the Golden Rule. There is no clearer example than the Jefferson Bible. Thomas Jefferson, the third president of the United States, published a book called *The Life and Morals of Jesus of Nazareth*, commonly referred to as the Jefferson Bible. Using a razor, he cut out sections of the four gospels (Matthew, Mark, Luke, John) and arranged them into a single narrative that he felt most accurately represented the teachings of Jesus. He excluded all elements of the supernatural, including the miracles of Jesus and his resurrection. He only had room for "facts." From this perspective, religion can only offer instruction on values and morals, nothing more.

Once the new rules of knowledge were established, more hacking took place. The inspiration and authority of the Bible fell onto the dissection table. Instead of reading the Word of God to understand and apply it, scholars evaluated, critiqued, and corrected it. When they were finished, they sent it to the corner of the library, to the shelf entitled "religious texts." It became one among many. Next to fall were any claims of personal interaction with the divine. People's subjective experiences could not be trusted. They could not be proven. They were suspicious at best and psychotic at worst.

In response many good-hearted Christians retreated from reason's roundtable discussion and set up camp outside of town. Movements like Pietism and revivalism were unsatisfied with the cold rationalism of Enlightenment Christianity, and thus tried to rekindle a fire for God in the hearts of believers through emotional and personal experience. And while this had some great successes, it came with a price. Intellectual territory was abandoned to the rationalists and spiritual territory was privatized. The disciplines of science and reason, which were once the prime stomping ground for Christian scholars, were viewed by many believers as dangerous to their faith. True Christian living, however, does not have to choose between the physical world and the spiritual world. The way forward involves both.

both eyes open

People who are committed to a materialistic worldview will never have room for God. Such people will rule out God from the beginning. They'll be operating with only one eye open. Even if they saw a "miracle," they could not by definition see it as supernatural. They would explain it as an operable law of nature that is not yet understood, or they would doubt their own subjective experiences, wondering if what they saw was a hallucination or mind trick. They cannot see God or his work because they have no room in their minds and hearts for him. They are faithful unbelievers and there is no convincing them.

People with both eyes wide open come to different conclusions. They may start with doubts; they might even start out atheistic; they might have a long list of questions addressed to God. But through their searching, they find answers. Their reason and experience lead them to something beyond themselves. They know better than to think they are the gods of this sphere. They know they cannot have infinite knowledge, that their eighty or so years on the earth will not be enough to discover all truth. Instead, they graciously accept the wisdom given to them by the One who is infinitely knowledgeable and eternal. They are open to God, and they find him. God makes sense to them. They recognize Christianity as the most logical belief system; all the pieces fit. They experience the thrill of having a purpose and the freedom of being united with someone bigger than themselves.

a train of ifs

Yes, Christianity is reasonable . . . if. It's reasonable if you don't rule out God from the start. It is reasonable if you don't think you are the highest authority on knowledge. It is reasonable if you are willing to include more evidence than just materialistic experimentation and logical argumentation. It is reasonable if there is a God who created the universe and therefore is not limited by its guiding principles (laws of nature) that he created in the first place. It is reasonable if you consider that history is not a repeatable experiment, and the miracles in the Bible cannot be replicated because they are unique acts of God. It is reasonable if you let reason and facts lead you in the direction they actually lead, even if that final destination confronts your original assumptions.

Let me ask a few questions.

1. Is there a God or not?

If you answer no, then you are a committed naturalist. You have set up criteria for truth that assumes there is no God. Even though it's impossible to prove there is no God, if you assume there is not, then you will remain a committed naturalist. However, if your answer is maybe or yes, then you are at least open to possibilities beyond the material universe. Good. Let's move to the second question.

2. If there might be a God, can I know that he exists or anything about him?

It's conceivable that a supernatural deity created us but is totally beyond our reach. In this case, no matter what we do, we cannot connect with this being. We're on our own, so there is no point in searching. The other option is that we can, to some degree, know about this divine being. Again, if your answer is maybe or yes, we can move on to the next question.

3. If I can know God, what is he like and how can I learn about him?

Christians believe there are two main ways we can know God or know about him. The first is natural revelation. This method employs the natural world, as well as human reason and experience. By observing the world, we can see order, design, purpose, and beauty. We can logically infer that this effect must have had a cause. This creation must have had a creator. Something doesn't come from nothing. The world, in all its variety and wonder, didn't just start to exist. This line of thinking points us to God or the fact that some creative being must exist. We can also observe in human beings things like love, virtue, conscience, rationality, sacrifice, desire for meaning, longing for relationship, and a hunger for truth. These attributes also point us to a creator who is reasonable, loving, just, or at least powerful enough to create these characteristics in humanity.

The second is divine revelation. If natural revelation is God showing himself through his created world, divine revelation is God showing himself through his specific personal involvement with humanity. He breaks the silence. God has revealed himself in a variety of ways throughout history, but his actions are always unique and personal. He acts within time and space. He relates to specific people in specific ways. Sometimes he speaks in an audible voice. Sometimes he reveals himself visually. Sometimes he speaks to the mind and heart without audible noises. Sometimes he demonstrates himself through acts of nature. All these kinds of divine revelation are recorded in the Bible. It is the big book of how God has related to humanity in history. The writers of the Bible saw, heard, or otherwise encountered God in their real world. They wrote about it. They wanted us to know and believe too.

The pinnacle of divine revelation is Jesus Christ. He is God's clearest message to humanity. If we want to know about God, we must look at Jesus. The four gospels are records of Jesus' teachings, miracles, death, resurrection, and ascension.

People still have encounters with God today. These encounters may happen through reading the Bible, hearing an audible voice, seeing a vision, or talking with another person. Sometimes it is an internal sense, inaudible but clear. God is still revealing himself to us today. He wants us to know him!

4. If the Bible is the book of God's self-revelation to the world, how can I know it is a trustworthy source?

There are several contributing factors. Archaeological discoveries verify biblical information. Other ancient texts provide historical confirmation. The biblical manuscripts were preserved with incredible precision and reliability through time. Jesus' miracles validated his claims, especially his death and resurrection. Several eyewitnesses wrote and confirmed their accounts of Jesus' life and miracles, as recorded in the Gospels and other ancient texts. Many of Jesus' followers were killed for their beliefs. The early Christian church grew rapidly, despite persecution and struggle. The gospel has had tremendous impact on the world for the last two millennia. And there is a large body of evidence that is growing today that reveals the truth of Jesus: changed lives. All of this evidence, though I've only scratched the surface, serves to support and confirm the Christian faith.

5. If the Bible gives accurate information about Jesus, what do I do about it?

Jesus does not simply teach moral rules. He brings a crisis. Paths really do diverge. Many people are convinced their one open eye is leading them in the right way, but they are blinded by their faith in themselves. Jesus calls out to anyone who will hear. We each have a choice about how we respond.

I have found solid answers to some of my own questions. For others I'm still searching for answers. There are still other questions that have no answers. They only lead deeper into the mystery of God. I can live with unanswered questions because it is these questions that fuel my quest. They drive me to explore and imagine. They cause me to press closer to God and listen intently to his whispers. I don't even think God will give me all the answers when I get to heaven. Maybe I don't need all the answers. Perhaps I'm often asking the wrong questions.

God wants us to know him. That much is possible for anyone. But we cannot figure him out. He is untamable, even by our best philosophies and theologies. He cannot be contained by categories of thought, proofs, or human reason. He is bigger than the buckets we try to carry him in. When we walk with God, there is no leash. We don't get to put a choker chain around his neck and drag him where we think he should go. And in his grace, he doesn't do that to us either. To walk with God requires faith. One definition of faith is to be sure of what you hope for and certain of what you can't see. That doesn't mean faith is blind; it means faith sees evidence the natural eye misses. When reason and science come to their limits, faith jumps off the dock and into the water. And then faith commits to swimming in the direction it believes to be true, even in the presence of doubts.

So which path seems more reasonable to you: the one where you figure out everything on your own, or the one where you follow the expert guide who created you?

questions for reflection

What does it mean to be a rational person?

How is your definition different from other definitions you've encountered?

Is Christianity the most reasonable belief system? Why or why not?

Have you heard other people tell stories of their experiences with God? Do you count this as evidence for God? Why or why not?

questions for action

Refer to your initial list from chapter 2. How many of the things on your list could be categorized as rational tensions?

Which of your rational questions or doubts do you need to spend more time reading and thinking about?

What books, people, or resources will you utilize to further explore your questions?

notes

1. "Justin Martyr," Christian History, accessed June 27, 2012, http://www.christianitytoday.com/ch/131christians/ evangelistsandapologists/martyr.html.

2. "Against Heresies," New Advent, accessed June 27, 2012, http://www.newadvent.org/fathers/0103100.htm.

3. "Quotations," accessed June 27, 2012, http://www.ter tullian.org/quotes.htm.

4. "De Principiis," New Advent, accessed June 27, 2012, http://www.newadvent.org/fathers/04121.htm.

5. St. Athanasius, *On the Incarnation of the Word of God: Being the Treatise of St. Athanusius, De Incarnatione Verbi Dei* (n.p.: Macmillan, 1954), accessed June 27, 2012, http://books. google.com/books?id=1Ux3a9kkCsMC&pg=PT26&lpg=PT2 6&dq=#v=onepage&q&f=false.

6. Saint Augustine, *Confessions*, trans. Henry Chadwick (Oxford: Oxford University Press, 1991), 3.

7. "The Immutability of God," accessed June 27, 2012, http://www.sacred-texts.com/chr/aquinas/summa/sum 012.htm.

7

evolution

bumper stickers at war

The symbol of a fish has long represented Christianity. It was used as a sort of secret code in ancient times of persecution. It remains today as a quick and easy signpost for Christians to recognize one another in society. Some Christians still have the symbol in their homes, on their business ads, or on their bumper stickers.

You can also see bumper stickers picturing a fish with legs. This "evolved fish" represents Darwin, or more accurately, the theory of evolution. The symbol is often displayed as a direct contradiction to the Christian fish. As a comic rendering of a caustic battle, sometimes one fish is eating the other.

I have never actually seen two people fist fighting over this debate. Nor have I seen one person trying to eat the other. But the bumper stickers are right. Like battleship flags, they remind us there is a war of ideas, and often the fish don't belong to the same "schools" of thought. There might not be enough room in the pond for both of them to survive.

bison killers

Several years ago, I spent a summer in Yellowstone National Park. It was a dream come true for me. My heart always comes alive in the forests, fields, and mountains. I am at home in the wild. That summer was like a long bath in a river of beauty. It filled my soul to overflowing and provided treasures of memories I will draw upon for a lifetime. My day job in the park began at 8:30 a.m., but I would wake up around 4:30 a.m. While it was still dark—the stars glimmering in the night—I would venture onto a hiking trail. I often went alone. This would be dangerous to do anywhere, but especially in an area known for its bears, wolves, bison, and moose. By the time the sun emerged over the mountainous landscape, I was usually deep in the backcountry. I can still feel the romance of the morning mist, the fading crescent moon above the towering pines, the explosion of hot geyser spouts, and the trepid footsteps of deer on the forest floor.

One morning my route passed by Morning Glory Pool. It is a deep well filled with scalding hot water. In the right light, the pool displays radiant hues of blues and greens—a glorious sight in the morning or anytime of the day. Wildflowers added to the surrounding spectrum of color. White. Yellow. Purple. All of them yearning to show their beauty. But that morning there was something unusual littering the path. It was a pile of bones—the discarded scraps of the bison killers. That's what the old-timers called the especially large and ferocious grizzly bears. The bears usually ate plants and smaller animals, but when that wasn't enough, these beasts would devour bison. If you have never seen a bison in the wild (they are commonly referred to as the American buffalo), picture a cow on steroids. Bison can weigh up to two thousand pounds and run up to thirty miles per hour. Both males and females have horns on their heads. Though generally passive, grazing creatures, they can be extremely aggressive when threatened. These were the prey of the grizzly bears. And the gigantic bones and tufts of hair remained to mark the success of the bears' hunt. As I stood there examining the remnants, imagining what the attack must have looked like, a slight fear crept up my spine. What if I encountered one of the bison killers on the trail today? Would I have a chance of survival, or would my remains be the next decaying landmark? It was a humbling moment. I was reminded that nature is as deadly as she is beautiful. The drama of life is no less than epic adventure, comedy, romance, and bloody horror in one script.

Excursions into the wild remind us that life is not safe, tame, or neatly packaged. It is a struggle to survive. These treks into nature also remind us that our planet is not a perfect place. We don't live in heaven. On earth living things eat each other. Life and death are dancing partners. Even those who are not interested in science cannot help but ask the basic questions of life: Where did all this come from? Why is life often so harsh? Is there any purpose to it all? Some scientists say that the theory of evolution answers those questions. Christians believe the Bible answers those questions. Are the answers the same? Are they even compatible? Or are they like bison versus grizzly? Can only one survive in the end?

simply stated

The general theory of evolution simply says that all living things came from a common ancestor. The original organism or organisms came from nonliving material. Evolutionary scientists say that the early earth contained inorganic (nonliving) ingredients that became a single-celled (living) organism. That single-celled organism multiplied and adapted to new environments over time to become multicellular organisms. Those organisms evolved into increasingly complex forms of life (like fish, birds, dinosaurs, monkeys, etc.). The mechanism for this evolution was natural selection. This is where nature preserves certain genetic mutations because they increase the organism's ability to survive. The genes most helpful to survival are passed on in reproduction. So over millions and millions of years and an array of genetic mutations, life has moved from an unthinking bacterium to an inquisitive book reader like yourself. Amazing, huh?

Let's look at a brief history of how this theory came into being. Then we will explore whether the two-legged fish really does gobble up the legless fish.

Modern science owes much to a belief in God and the Bible. The belief that God created the universe and God is orderly gave early Western scientists confidence to explore the universe and discover orderly principles. Revolutionaries like Galileo Galilei, Francis Bacon, and Isaac Newton were all under that impression. While sometimes at odds with the political powers of the church, these men and many others experimented, hypothesized, and theorized from a worldview in which God was creator (though they did not always maintain orthodox Christian beliefs).

As we saw in the previous chapter, the Enlightenment fought for a system based on reason and experience. Science was a key player in this enterprise. But it was hard to rule out God when you believed that he created the world. Charles Darwin helped to oust the scientific necessity for a creator and therefore closed the loop of philosophical naturalism. He did this by explaining the origins of the universe in naturalistic terms.

Darwin was baptized in the Anglican Church. His family intended for him to become a minister, but instead he ended up on a ship to the Galapagos Islands, where he conceived his world-changing idea. His two main works, *The Origin of Species* and *The Descent of Man*, explain his evolutionary ideas in great length.

Darwin's theory was met with much praise and as much criticism in the early days. But if we fast forward to the present, it has won over the scientific imagination and seems to be the floorboards on which science moves. However, there is no unanimous opinion about it. Scientists, scholars, theologians, and you and me have many thoughts on the subject. I will sketch out four basic ways to interpret the theory of evolution and how it relates to Christian faith.

atheistic evolution

This view says that there is no supernatural being. The only thing that exists is the material world. The world is a closed system, and nature functions predictably within it. There is only the natural eye, so gouge out the spiritual one—it's a fantasy.

From this perspective, the theory of evolution is fact, and it proves concretely that there is no God. Someone who believes this position might say something like:

The earth is over four billion years old. At one time, our planet did not have any living things on it. It only had certain atmospheric conditions and elemental ingredients that made life possible. When the conditions were just right, the existing material combined to make a simple form of organic life. And that simple single-celled organism multiplied. Every time a living thing multiplies or reproduces, it has the possibility for slight genetic changes called mutations. These mutations cause the "child" to be slightly different than the "parent." Sometimes one child is better at surviving than her siblings, so she is able to mate and have children, and pass on her genetic material— including the mutation that made her more likely to survive. This is natural selection, and it has been happening for millions of years starting with that first single-celled life-form. Mutations brought on increasing complexity and eventually new species. The species spread out all over the world, and continued to evolve into all the diverse forms of life we have today, including humans. We didn't exactly come from apes, but we came from the same common ancestor as apes. So it is clear that nothing was created by God. The idea of God is a myth that was created by primitive humans to give them comfort and meaning. The truth is, humans are just like all other forms of life. We evolved from a common ancestor. The process had no purpose or design. It was without direction or destination. We just happened. There is no afterlife. There are no miracles. Your suffering and pain are a result of natural causes, and there is no point to it. You will eventually die, and then that's it.

There are other branches of thought within this perspective that could be considered agnostic. An agnostic says there is no way to know whether or not God exists, but we can explain the world without him. Charles Darwin identified himself in this category toward the end of his life.

theistic evolution

Theistic evolution is an attempt to synthesize the theory of evolution with a belief in God. It holds to the same basic story as atheistic evolution, except it says that God is behind it all. God used evolution as the process to create the world. Someone from this perspective might say:

God existed before anything else. He caused the big bang. He implemented the process of evolution and let it unfold over many millennia. He probably intervened at key points to guide the process. The evolutionary evidence does not contradict Scripture; it only contradicts some interpretations of Scripture. The Bible's intent was to tell the story of redemption, not to make scientific or historical claims about the origins of life.

Theistic evolutionists maintain that God created the universe, but they look to evolution to explain how he did it. Unlike atheistic evolutionists who argue that the process is unguided and random, theists would say that God gave direction to the course of evolution. This position faces several areas of challenge. It can reduce the connection between empirical evidence and the reality of God's handiwork in creation. It raises questions about the image of God in humans as distinct from earlier non-human ancestors. It requires theological adjustments regarding the doctrine of sin and an explanation for the bloody and long process required for nature to produce sentient beings. Still, many Christian groups officially espouse theistic evolution and continually seek to wrestle with the connections of the Bible and scientific research.

intelligent design

This perspective says that scientific exploration produces significant evidence that the world and its inhabitants were designed by an intelligent agent. This view does not necessarily provide a holistic faith story or even require any connections with the Bible. It begins with observation and experimentation to show that life is better explained by a designer with intelligent action than by evolutionary chance. Someone from this perspective might say:

Life-forms on Earth do evolve and change, but the theory of evolution doesn't jive with the evidence science is producing. A better theory is that the earth and the life it contains was created on purpose by an intelligent being. It makes no sense rationally or empirically to say that an intelligent creature like human beings originated from a mindless material source. The fine-tuning of nature, the organization of genetic information, the complexity of even life's simplest organisms, and the probabilities involved all point directly toward a designer.

Intelligent design research is being done by scientists who often fail to gain a serious hearing in the public forum. It is often dismissed as a religious agenda masquerading in scientific sheepskins. Though there *are* personal spiritual implications of the theory, these don't automatically disqualify its scientific validity. If God really did create the world, shouldn't we be able to find some clues of his handiwork? If the natural eye and spiritual eye really do work together to bring the world into clearer focus, then science and faith are not at odds.

creation science

This perspective begins with the Bible as its starting point for scientific inquiry. Scientific evidence is then plotted along the timeline of the Christian meta-narrative. While interpreting the Bible more literally, creation science seeks to integrate faith and fact directly and logically. Someone from this perspective might say:

God really did create the world as revealed in the Bible. Some say the world is relatively young; others say it is much older. The main point is that God created various "kinds" of living things. Humanity was a separate kind from the other creatures. Noah brought a pair of each kind onto the ark, so there were relatively few ancestral kinds that existed in his time. The flood wiped out most other land animals, and the survivors from the ark spread out into the world and diversified into the life-forms we experience today. There are no contradictions between the Bible and scientific evidence, only unsolved puzzles and perhaps unsolvable mysteries.

This view has often been criticized harshly by proponents of the first two perspectives above. Though creation science advocates, as well as intelligent design proponents, have attempted to include their views in public school curriculum, they have been largely unsuccessful. This is partly attributed to a growing redefinition in the philosophy of science.

a faith story with a few facts

What are the limits of science? How large is its territory? Lately, some scientists seem to have the Alexander the Great complex. They've been conquering foreign land and calling it their own. In other words, the theory of evolution—when used as a meta-narrative to disprove God's existence—is a faith story peppered with scientific facts. There are a bunch of dots in ink that are then connected with a pencil to form the shape the person originally expected to find. Dots that don't fit are maneuvered until they appear to fit. Dots that are missing are simply sketched in. (If you find this hard to believe, check into things like Haeckel's embryo chart, Darwin's tree of life, and the peppered moths photograph.)

The point is science is about observation, experimentation, hypothesis, and theory. It is scientific to observe the variations between skeletal structures of fossilized animals. It is unscientific to say that God does not exist based on a body of fossil evidence. It is scientific to observe the cause and effect between stepping into a lake and getting a wet foot. It is unscientific to conclude that Jesus did not walk on water. The theory of evolution—even if it is verified by as much scientific fact as many claim—does not provide any solid conclusions regarding God. It is no help in guiding our faith. It doesn't offer us the narrow path to life or prohibit us from walking it.

The theory of evolution with its closed system is a story with lots of guesses. For example, let's look at the beginning—origins cosmology. Where did Earth come from? Or where did the raw materials that formed the universe come from? Without the possibility of a higher power, the issue of the origin of the universe is a question mark. And once the raw inorganic materials were there, how did they suddenly become a living cell? Not sure. The best that can be done is to describe the components of life, but without explaining the transformation of nonliving to living. You may have heard claims about creating life in the laboratory, but those experiments have been largely discredited.

It is also unclear how the limited genetic material of a simple organism could increase its genetic material, processes, and organization to become a complex organism. Or how natural selection could favor slight mutations in larger mammals when mutations are generally harmful to the creature. Or how consciousness arose. But evolutionary science still goes on connecting the dots with pencil lines, then tracing over them with permanent marker, and ending up with a closed natural system with no room for God. We are left with a devastating story. The conclusions we draw from this evolutionary narrative are so horrific that I wonder if its believers have really felt the impact of their beliefs.

The path Jesus taught leads to full and complete life on the earth. This means joyful and meaningful days, a vibrant connection with the creator, and a corrected disposition toward others. And it means eternal life after our bodies die. That sounds like a great ending to a cosmic adventure story. Now contrast that story with the evolutionary faith narrative. In this new story, we have no idea where we come from. So when we ask the question, "Who are we?" we can only offer empty descriptions. We are a collection of cells arranged in a highly complex way to form a self-aware species. But there is no purpose to any of it. No purpose at the cellular level. No purpose throughout history. No purpose for our lives. No purpose in our marriages. No purpose in our work. Just bald existence and survival. Sorry to disappoint the world, but nobody is special. Our lives are meaningless. Our beliefs are fabrications. Our actions are arbitrary and genetically contrived. There is no ethical standard for living—it's a human social construct. We will all inevitably die and cease to exist. And when we do, the world will keep on spinning in a biological process without direction or destination.

Who could live like that?

areas of interest

Science interests me. I marvel at the starry sky at night. I'm exhilarated by the speed of a cheetah. I'm curious about how the mountains were formed. I like reading about how stranded iguanas adapt to new environments. But I am not an expert in any scientific field. It can be incredibly complex, even confusing. Maybe you've heard the old saying, "I refuse to have a battle of wits with an unarmed person." The same could be said of evolution: "I refuse to have a scientific debate with an uninformed person." I sometimes wonder if there are any scientists who are qualified to debate the topic. Is there anyone out there who can tout the proper credentials? Who has advanced degrees and extensive research experience in molecular biology, paleontology, geology, genetics, physics, chemistry, astronomy, embryology, and the list goes on.

Certainly, we should listen to real scientists and have informed opinions supported by credible sources. We should read broadly and deeply to the best of our abilities. But the reality is that most people will never pursue a PhD in anything, let alone biology. Most people don't even read one nonfiction book per month, let alone an academic work on the latest scientific research. So how can we make informed decisions based on the limitations that real life offers us?

I would suggest that if you are truly searching and wrestling through this evolution issue, then read a lot. Read authors from differing perspectives. Go to websites. Watch documentaries. Talk to scientists. Think for yourself and explore. But don't give up on Jesus in the process. Don't go through a freshman biology class in college and then make a lifelong decision to drift away from your faith. The consequences are too severe, and the topic is too important.

As a brief introduction, I'm going to mention some of the areas of interest you'll find as you delve into the issue of evolution and creation.

evolution in miniature

Evolutionists often say we can see the process happening right before our eyes—examples include virus mutations and evolution in fish populations. Indeed organisms do change and adapt to their environment. Even if they evolve into what science might classify as a new species, we cannot extrapolate backwards and assume that all life is like a tree that traces back to a single seed.

fossil records

A lot of emphasis has been placed on finding missing links in the fossil record—fossils that will clearly demonstrate the intermediaries between one distinct species and another. More fossils are being discovered every day, and many of them are held up as obvious intermediaries, sometimes with a bit of guesswork and artistic imagination.

genetics

This field of study had not yet been discovered at the time of Darwin. The complexities of DNA and how parts are assembled to make an organism has offered strong evidence that something or someone organized this information and designed its patterns of assembly. This is an important area of study for intelligent design theorists.

molecular biology

Microbiologist Michael Behe has written extensively to demonstrate that the theory of evolution falls apart under the microscope. He explains that the single-celled flagellum has working parts so complex that there is no way it could have been randomly derived by small, incremental mutations. All the pieces fit together and work perfectly, and it had to be that way from the start to work at all. The process of slow and gradual mutation is not a plausible theory for the intricately designed machinery found in living cells.

astronomy

Scientists have noticed that life on Earth requires many precise conditions to survive—everything from distance from the sun to specific concentrations of elements in the atmosphere to precise gravitational pull. Our planet is extremely fine-tuned to support life. It's evident from our knowledge of other planets and stars that life is unique. It makes more sense to say God created this with great precision than to say nature randomly arrived at these conditions.

other reasons

There are also reasons of the heart. My hopes and dreams have no toleration for a naturalistic worldview. I believe that life means something, that my actions matter and so do yours. I want a great adventure to live for. To believe in the theory of evolution with all its materialistic implications would be a fatal blow to my heart, a crushing defeat to my loving relationships, and a disappointing life indeed. Something inside me tells me there's more.

cling tightly

Most of us can afford to not know everything about science, but we cannot afford to remain indecisive about our lives. Research is constantly yielding new insights. Old theories are adjusted or trashed. Many of nature's puzzles are yet to be solved. Amidst all this, we can have faith while still seeking further understanding, and we can trust the person of Christ.

When I was in the middle of my faith crisis, most of my beliefs and doctrines crumbled to the ground. Only a few stones remained intact. I decided to believe those few ideas with everything in me. I chose them. They would stand tall amidst the rubble of my spiritual deconstruction. I called those beliefs my naked creed. They were what was left after my soul weathered the storm. The creed went something like this: "I believe that God created the world, and Jesus is who he said he is." This simple statement was the cornerstone on which I began to rebuild my faith. It survived the assault of my doubts and questions. And I decided to cling to this simple faith in Jesus no matter what.

You don't have to have all the answers, but you should know what you will die for. The earliest Christians did. They developed a saying that became known as the Apostle's Creed. It was their bottom line, their naked creed. It held the essentials, and they were written in blood.

We have been on this quest for several chapters now—the quest to find life on the right path. There are many unknowns along the way. Do you know what you believe? What is your naked creed?

the apostle's creed

I believe in God, the Father Almighty,
Maker of heaven and earth;

And in Jesus Christ, his only Son, our Lord:
who was conceived by the Holy Spirit,
born of the Virgin Mary,
suffered under Pontius Pilate,
was crucified, dead, and buried;
he descended into hell.

The third day he arose again from the dead;
he ascended into heaven,
and sits at the right hand of God the Father Almighty;
from there he shall come to judge the living and the dead.

I believe in the Holy Spirit, the holy catholic Church,
the communion of saints, the forgiveness of sins, the
resurrection of the body, and the life everlasting.

Amen.

questions for reflection

What evidence in nature have you seen for creation? For evolution?

How does your belief about how the world was created affect your personal life?

How does the Bible explain the violence and struggle seen in the natural world? How does the evolutionary story explain this?

questions for action

Read Genesis 1–3. Summarize the main message of these chapters. What are they telling you?

What questions regarding creation and evolution do you want to explore further?

Rowing harder
doesn't help if the
boat is headed in
the wrong direction.

—Kenichi Ohmae

8

relativism

across the seas

I sat on the beach one foggy morning staring out into the
South China Sea. I intended to read my Bible but spent more
time enjoying the cool breeze. A young Chinese man, a fellow
student at the university where I studied, approached me. We
introduced ourselves and began talking. He quickly became
my first real Chinese friend, and I his best *MeiGuo ren pengyou*
(American friend). His name was Chang. I steered our discussion
toward the Bible I was carrying and asked him, in English, if
he knew about Jesus. His puzzled expression told me that he
didn't. But he seemed curious, so I tried to explain. His English
abilities, though far superior to my Chinese speaking talents,
were fairly limited. So I began to search for a way to translate

the idea of God and Christ. I focused on the word *Shang Di*. I heard this was the word for God. But as I began speaking about *Shang Di*, I started to wonder if this god I was referring to was anything like the God of the Bible. What did the word mean in Chinese? What kind of god? These confusions caused us both to abort the discussion rather quickly without gaining any real clarity. But our friendship continued.

Later that month, I made more Chinese friends. I became involved with a break-dance crew. We spent a lot of time training at the studio and hanging around at parties. These guys were cool by every definition. And I was cool by association! Despite the language barrier, they welcomed me in and treated me like one of their own. From their influence, I grew as a dancer, and I learned more about life. It didn't take me long to realize that my new friends were not Christians. Most of them had nominal religious backgrounds. Some considered themselves Buddhists; others were agnostics. Instead of trying to translate the gospel to them myself, I decided to invite them to an underground Chinese church. Two of them cordially accepted the invitation, and I was excited for them to hear about Jesus.

My enthusiasm quickly diminished. Compared to their hip-hop lifestyle, this church seemed like a snooze. The pianist played clunky American hymns in English, singing all twelve verses, and then repeating them. The preacher put one of my friends to sleep. The outing seemed to be a complete failure. But they were polite, and the next day at the studio was the same as the day before.

That's when I started stewing about hell. I grew up believing that everyone who was not a Christian would go to hell when they die and burn forever. This belief was a lot easier to maintain when almost everyone I knew was a Christian, and everyone I'd ever met had certainly been to church and heard the message of the gospel. But now I was the foreigner, surrounded by millions of people who did not know about Jesus. They had never asked for Christ's forgiveness. They burned incense at the temple just like their parents and grandparents. Many who went away to college were converted to the religion of the academy: atheism. They learned, as many young adults do in America, that spirits are myths and that the only real god is human knowledge.

My faith was thrown into crisis. Was God really going to cast these millions, including my new friends, into the lake of fire where they would burn forever? I could not bear the thought. I began to wonder if I could believe in or love that kind of a God.

war and tolerance

History has given us many examples of how bad it can be when religions collide. In Western history, animosity between Christians and Muslims has led to much violence and bloodshed over many generations. Christians have even warred against other Christians over differing beliefs—drowning, burning, hanging, and slicing one another in an attempt to defend their faith. These large-scale conflicts are also reflected locally: the church that is hostile to the neighboring synagogue or even the neighboring Christian church; the Muslim man who belittles his atheist coworker; the kid at the lunch table who mocks her classmate for saying a prayer before she eats. Is it any wonder there are company regulations that forbid employees to talk about religion at work? Is it a surprise that people avoid talking to strangers who knock on their door asking spiritual questions? Amidst the chaos of religious battles, tolerance swept in and issued martial law to restore the mayhem to harmony. And tolerance has a professional guidance counselor called relativism.

The United States of America is one of the most religiously tolerant nations that has ever existed. From mainly Protestant and Catholic immigrant populations, it has grown into a diverse jungle, flowering with every kind of belief. People from every part of the world have come to America looking for greater opportunities. And they brought with them not only their culture, but also their religion. If you take a driving tour around the country, you will see monuments of the religious ingredients that have been added to the melting pot: Mormon temples, gothic cathedrals, Buddhist monasteries, Christian Science reading rooms, Quaker chapels, Muslim mosques. We live in a land of religious diversity.

Tolerance has emerged as the magic method to help us all get along. It's a good idea, isn't it? It's much better to respect your agnostic cousin than to convert him or her by threat of violence. It is much better to let the mosque and the church exist as centers of worship rather than staging points for community combat. Every person bears God's image. We are all worthy of respect, even those who don't act respectably. However, that divine image in us does not automatically mean that our doctrines and decisions are right or respectable. Religious wars are abysmal. Religious tolerance is amiable. But something else is needed: truth and love.

war of cultures

Sometimes fights between different religions are more like culture conflicts. Though religious beliefs and cultural norms are distinct, they are often so tightly knit together that it is hard to tell them apart. A lot of conflict comes from customs rather than beliefs. For example, it is easy to feel distanced from someone because of his or her clothing, food, color of skin, or strange sounding language. Because people of drastically different cultures often do not share the same religion, it is easy to lump everything together and associate a certain ethnicity with a certain belief system. This is a mistake and one that missionaries in the past often made. In the early days of foreign missions, white Westerners from Europe and America often sent their white missionaries into distant lands to share the gospel. Unfortunately, the missionaries sometimes brought along their culture as part of the essence of Christianity. They did not yet understand enculturation.

God always translates himself to us. He is too great for us to comprehend by ourselves, so he takes steps to show himself to us in ways we can grasp. For example, the Bible is written in a human language. The original manuscripts were written in three languages: Hebrew, Greek, and Aramaic. When God spoke to people like Moses, he spoke in a language Moses could understand. And Moses retold the message in a way the people could understand. Jewish prophets wrote their messages in a language the readers would comprehend (Hebrew). The gospel writers wrote in a discernable language. God even translated himself into a form that we could understand— a man.

Jesus is God's ultimate example of enculturation. God himself became human and entered a particular culture at a particular point in history. Jesus spoke a common language with his neighbors, wore the same kinds of clothes, and ate the same kinds of food. Is that because God was confined to the culture of Nazareth? No, but he took shape within it. It's like filling a cup with water from the ocean. Does that mean the ocean is now the same thing as the cup? No. The cup holds the water, and even then it does not prevent it from taking shape in other containers.

The gospel always exists within a particular culture. There is no pure culture that perfectly reflects the kingdom of God. God makes his dwelling in any human heart that will receive him, regardless of ethnicity. This is important for us to remember when we discuss relativism. Christianity is not the same thing as the particular culture it lives in. Not all of my Chinese friends are Buddhists. Not all Chinese are non-Christians. In fact, the church is growing by leaps and bounds in China, much more than it is in the United States. And there are many Americans who dress nicely, behave morally, have an education, drive new cars, maybe even go to church, but are far from being Christian. We tend to judge by the outward appearance, but God looks at the heart (see 1 Samuel 16:7).

sociology and your satanic neighbor

In recent years, we have amassed quite a bit of knowledge about cultures around the world. Some academic researchers spend their entire careers doing field work with a particular people group. Comparative studies on religion have emerged from this kind of work. One point has become evident: People believe many different things! Certainly not everyone believes that Jesus is the Savior of the world. Some people embrace everything as a god; some people aren't that interested in gods at all. Yet sociologists have found common themes in many cultures throughout history and have often drawn the wrong conclusions. For example, most people groups have some kind of belief in a higher power. The naturalistic (evolutionary) theory would say religious belief is a useful survival mechanism, despite the fact that it is a fantasy, and that is why it has been preserved among humans of diverse cultures thus far. Many also teach that while no one particular religion is universally true, all have value and truth in their context.

Relativism means that all beliefs are valid. Truth is relative to your environment, circumstance, and community. Relativism allows for mutually exclusive beliefs to coexist by making them both impotent regarding historical and universal truth. Instead, we are left with little chunks of truth that are helpful and meaningful. These little truths add value to our lives, but they are not permitted to gobble up another person's truths. They must stay in their own individualistic realm and never claim to apply to everyone everywhere. So if you are a Christian and your neighbor is a Satanist, you must both peacefully coexist. Your Christian beliefs add value to your life, and his satanic beliefs add value to his life. Neither belief can claim truth that extends onto the other neighbor's property.

Religious beliefs are reduced to communal creations. Society sets the standard. If reality is relative and truth is based on the situation, we need not appeal to a higher authority but to the masses. Perhaps this is why the polling of public opinion has become so popular. Fifty-six percent of Americans believe this. Eighty-two percent believe that. Is this more often a survey of opinions or a truth-seeking census? What happens when Truth with a capital T is no longer allowed? Well, anything goes. Anything except intolerance.

is there truth?

Is something true because you believe it, or do you believe it because it's true? The fact that I believe the Christian story doesn't make it true, and it doesn't make it true for me. I believe the Christian story because it is already true. It will still be true whether I believe it or not. Jesus said he is not only the way and the life, but also the truth. What contradicts Jesus is not another truth; it is falsehood.

Relativism is logically inconsistent. Its basic premise is that all truth is relative. But if all truth is truly relative, one cannot make an absolute statement like, "All truth is relative." That statement would then also have to be relative. Strict relativists are big on tolerance. They advocate for people of different beliefs to tolerate one another. They get upset at Christians who say there is a truth that applies to everyone.

Jesus spoke often about truth. He said things like, "If you hold to my teaching, you are really my disciples. Then you will know the truth, and the truth will set you free" (John 8:31–32). "When he, the Spirit of truth, comes, he will guide you into all truth" (John 16:13). Jesus knew his statements about truth, especially those about him being the Son of God, would cause friction. They got him killed.

The early followers of Jesus were bold in teaching that the truth of Christianity was not a local fad or a privatized religious sect. They were committed, even to the point of death, to bringing the truth of Jesus to all people everywhere. Consider their own words:

- "That which was from the beginning, which we have heard, which we have seen with our eyes, which we have looked at and our hands have touched—this we proclaim concerning the Word of life. The life appeared; we have seen it and testify to it, and we proclaim to you the eternal life, which was with the Father and has appeared to us. We proclaim to you what we have seen and heard, so that you also may have fellowship with us. And our fellowship is with the Father and with his Son, Jesus Christ" (1 John 1:1–3).

- "I am not ashamed of the gospel, because it is the power of God for the salvation of everyone who believes: first for the Jew, then for the Gentile" (Romans 1:16).

- "Therefore go and make disciples of all nations, baptizing them in the name of the Father and of the Son and of the Holy Spirit, and teaching them to obey everything I have commanded you. And surely I am with you always, to the very end of the age" (Matthew 28:19–21).

The Bible contains a meta-narrative. It is the big story of the universe into which all other stories fit or don't fit. It is not a compilation of myths to inspire morality; it is a sweeping view of all reality. The Christian message is that God really did create the world, that human sin destroys our relationships with God, that Jesus truly is the Son of God, and that he was born on the earth as a baby. He lived in a particular place (Nazareth) at a particular time (the beginning of the first century A.D.). He had real students (the disciples) who wrote real accounts of his life teachings (the Gospels). He was crucified on a real cross; he died and was buried for three days. Then he rose from the dead. God brought Jesus from death to life. Jesus met with many of his followers after the resurrection. Then he ascended to heaven where he is alive and waiting for God's signal to return to the earth and bring human history to a dramatic conclusion. Our lives are being lived in the middle of this story. We each face a personal decision: What will we believe, and how will we live?

No other belief system says the same thing as Christianity. They are all different by varying degrees. If all the stories can't be true, how is a Christian to interpret other religions? Are other belief systems carefully crafted lies of the Devil intended to lead humanity away from Jesus? Are other religions misguided derivatives from the one true story? Or are they human constructs seeking to feed our basic hunger for meaning and hope? I would venture to say that perhaps all three of those possibilities are at play. If there really is a true narrative that we desperately need to know, then it would seem that our human quest for God could lead us to some misconceptions like pantheism or agnosticism. It also seems that creating a pseudo-story such as atheism would be a good strategy for the Enemy of our souls to sell to us. After all, in this story of Christianity, there is an Enemy. He is at war with God, and he is at war with God's most treasured creation—us.

dodge the draft or grab a gun?

Unnecessary religious carnage is just what tolerance is trying to avoid. Yet here we are, talking about war again. But not a war that takes ignorant shots at strange-looking foreigners. This time it's shoot to kill and at the right targets. We are in a battle. The truth of Jesus is in conflict. It is, in one sense, a war of worlds. The kingdom of God is invading the kingdom of the earth. The world we live in is enemy-occupied territory. The enemy is not the Muslim or the Jew. The enemy is the Devil. He has been God's unequal adversary since before the world was created. His mission is the opposite of Jesus' mission. Jesus wants to bring us life; the Devil wants to destroy it. The Devil as an idea has been cartoon-ized and Halloween-ized to such a degree that the discussion of him almost seems childish and embarrassing. He has been officially stricken from the record as it relates to almost every academic arena, including many theological teachings. Many Americans view the Devil as an outdated, third-world, unrealistic personification of what is wrong with humanity.

Is the Devil a bygone fantasy? Scripture certainly indicates he is real. Jesus clearly believes there is a Devil. If there are real spiritual forces of evil loose in our world, the war of ideas and religions begins to look a little bit more serious. And the pencil sketch of our enemy gets a little clearer. Paul said, "We are not fighting against flesh-and-blood enemies, but against evil rulers and authorities of the unseen world, against mighty powers in this dark world, and against evil spirits in the heavenly places" (Ephesians 6:12 NLT). His conclusion? It was not to avoid the war and hide out in spiritual safe havens. He said to strap on every piece of armor available to us so we can resist our Enemy. None of these pieces of armor includes a weapon with which to kill someone of a different faith. There is no "sword of conversion." We are not instructed to badger the unbeliever into the kingdom of God or told to assault the atheist with cogent apologetics. We are given armor for spiritual adversaries; we are not fighting against our physical friends of different beliefs. Our strategy of engaging those of other religions is not warfare; it's prayer. Then while we pray, we can listen, love, and share how God has been real in our lives. Then keep praying.

Our collective role against dark forces is active resistance. Our collective role with those of differing beliefs is more like being salt and light. God throws us into the middle of the decaying lives of others so that we can be agents of renewal, like salt on meat before the days of refrigeration. It is our light, the example of our lives, that gives hope and direction to others who are searching for God. So in this war, the lives of the unbelievers are at stake. My desire is not to see them crushed by the hand of God, but rescued by him.

heaven and hell

Heaven and hell seem to be the bottom line in our thinking. We can discuss evangelistic techniques or compare doctrines, but doesn't it all boil down to who gets into heaven and who goes to hell? Like the idea of the Devil, many have jettisoned a belief in hell, partially because the thought is too painful to bear. Can you imagine your spouse, sibling, child, or parent trapped in torment and flames forever? If this is what Jesus teaches, wouldn't this be a good time to turn and walk away? Could a God who sends people to hell be considered loving by any definition? And who could follow him? It is much easier on our consciences to blot out the concept of hell and go on believing in a loving and merciful God. We would do anything and go to any length—rearrange the Bible stories, refuse to believe the Bible, reject God—to avoid dealing with hell. And that's exactly how God feels.

God would go to any length and do anything—even die— so that we could escape the reality of hell. This is the message of Jesus. It's supposed to be good news. We'd rather erase the idea of punishment, but with it would go God's justice. This won't work, since God is not a Mr. Potato Head we can reconstruct as we wish. To wrestle with this reality, we need a bigger understanding of God; then we'll see more clearly how each of our lives has a destination.

Before worrying about hell, let's think about God. His defining characteristic is love. There is deep love shared between the Father, Son, and Spirit. That love extends to each person who has ever lived. We are God's children. He created us to love us and for us to love him back. This sounds pretty good so far. How does it take a turn for the worse? By our choices. For love to be real, it must be optional. It wouldn't be true love if God made us do it. We would be a piece of machinery, engineered to perform a specific function without conscious choice. God gave us the freedom to love him or leave him. Humanity chose to leave right from the start. It has become a kind of first nature for us to reject God's love instead of reaching for it. God can go to any length to love us, but it's our own personal choice whether we receive and reciprocate that love.

Justice is another core part of who God is. He doesn't create some arbitrary standard and slap it onto the world, telling us to follow a set of rules. Instead, he is just. He is right. Wrong is what is contrary to him. Injustice exists, but God cannot let it reign unchecked or unresolved. We immediately see the need for some kind of corrective measure here. You and I have a strong sense of justice too. We cringe at the thought of a serial killer remaining at large. We hate to see a rapist go free based on a legal loophole. We get angry when the bully steals the smaller kid's lunch money. Or when the car mechanic charges us too much for a repair. We crave justice! Often we get angry at God for not bringing justice. We ask him to restore our destroyed reputations. We want him to punish the people who hurt us. We want him to expose the hypocrites. We want him to kill the killers. And then, in an ironic reversal, we blame God for being unloving when we begin to talk about eternal punishment, accusing him of being too harsh. Our prayers might go something like this: "God, I want justice, and I want it now. I'll tell you what it should look like. But I don't want people to burn in hell forever."

I don't want people to burn in hell forever. Do you? God doesn't either. Will anyone burn in hell forever?

God's justice

The warnings are real. They are not to be ignored. Jesus said the broad road would lead to destruction (Matthew 7:13).

He said the weeds would be pulled out and thrown into the fire, while the wheat would be harvested (Matthew 13:24–30). He said the wicked servant will be cut up into many pieces (Luke 12:42–46). He said some will be thrown out into the streets that are filled with weeping (Matthew 22:1–14). The book of Revelation paints a portrait of a final battle where Satan and his soldiers are defeated with one swift move from God. Then all the enemies of God are thrown into the lake of fire to be burned forever (Revelation 19—20). Our choices have serious consequences—eternal consequences. We may not see justice enacted as quickly as we'd like, but God promises to bring each person to perfect justice at the end.

I believe that God's justice is better than mine. Like any court judge, I would only make judgments based on limited information. God sees everything. He knows our hearts. He's had intimate knowledge of every thought, word, and secret activity we've ever had. To think that God knows us so precisely makes me a little nervous. I don't know if I want to be judged by someone who knows everything about me. God will not have a biased opinion against certain people, nor will he throw down a harsh sentence to someone who doesn't deserve it. He will bring perfect justice to each person. I know I can't do this.

Is it ever perfect justice for some people to spend eternity in hell? The Bible seems to say yes. One definition of hell is separation from God forever. He is all that is good and to live without him would be ultimate misery. Since we are eternal beings, we are going to live forever one way or another. There are people in this world who totally reject God for their whole lives. Why is it unreasonable to think that they could totally reject God for eternity? In that case, God gives them what they choose—a life without him. Some have said the gates of hell are locked from the inside. I think this is at least partially true.

God's mercy

I shudder for those who minimize God's justice, and I weep for those who minimize his mercy. In the mystery of God, these two attributes coalesce instead of collide. It is not our job to enforce them, and it is not for us to eradicate either one. God's love is legendary. He has taken even the worst of men and women into his arms and welcomed them into his heart. He is not surprised by our disobedience. He already took care of that when Jesus paid for it on the cross. His affection extends to everyone. He comes to us ready to forgive our sins and make us his own again. Our part is vital, but very simple. We accept his love and let it change us.

I cannot judge who goes to heaven or hell. Neither can you. It is not our place. God, and only God, can do it. As I trust in God's justice, I also trust in his mercy. I don't believe he is going to be cruel or indifferent when it comes to the people he created, loves, and died for. I wonder if many of us will be surprised by some of the people we encounter in heaven. People who we were sure would not be there. People we would have condemned forever. People who didn't fit into our formulas.

But what about the remote island peoples who have never heard the gospel? What about infants who died? What about those who lived before the time of Christ? What about faithful Muslims? What about my uncle Joe who never went to church but lived a good life? You have no power to judge or save them. Entrust them into God's mercy. Your responsibility is with those who are still alive. You might not be clear about where particular people have gone when they died, but two things are very clear: (1) God wants everyone to have a life-changing relationship with him through Jesus Christ, and (2) God wants you to help them have it.

Many of my questions about heaven and hell are not yet answered. But I know how to live, and where I'm going when I die. I know the basics of what God wants for each person. And I can take part in that process.

God wants everyone to understand the big-picture story about creation, the fall, and redemption. He wants us to give our lives to Jesus and to let him be in charge. He wants us to ask for forgiveness from our sins and leave our old sinful lives behind. It is clear that God wants everyone to trust in Jesus and follow him on the narrow path that leads to life. It might be unclear to us who has actually begun that journey or how far along they are and how far forgiveness really does extend. Without dismissing the reality of eternal justice, I quietly hope that God's mercy has much longer arms than we imagine.

The narrow road is not just for you and me either. God wants everyone to be safe. He doesn't want anyone plodding down the road to destruction. His love is still calling out like a song in the night. Those who are lost might hear his voice but struggle to navigate through the darkness to find their way home. We can take them by the hand and lead them to Jesus. If you have given your life to Jesus, you know the way home. All the people in your life are walking somewhere. They've chosen a path, whether they realize it or not. Maybe some of them are headed toward disaster. Maybe you could make a difference in their lives forever.

humble to the core

Christians believe that there is one story that connects all people. We believe truth has a name: Jesus. There are many friendly, well-intentioned people who believe differently. They are not our enemies. They are people whom God loves. They are worthy of respect and dignity. Relativism would eliminate the critical differences between different religions. Christ compels us to follow one path. His desire is that all people would find life in him. The fact that Christians have found it does not mean that we think we're better than anyone else. What a disappointment that kind of attitude would be to Jesus, and such a disgrace to his character. As Martin Luther reportedly wrote right before he died, we are all simply beggars. We are humbly telling other beggars where we have found bread.

The horrors of life without God are outmatched by the brilliance of eternal life with him. We have the hope of life in the fullest sense of the word. We are offered only glimpses of what this eternal life will be like: a reunion with our Christian friends and family, a dream come true, a tear wiped away, being next-door neighbors with God himself. Jesus is already there; now he waits to welcome us. His hope is that no one would wander off, but that every person, even those whose faith has been jaded by the crossfire of life, would find their way home.

questions for reflection

Where have you seen examples of relativism in action?

Have you seen Christians warring against people with different beliefs instead of loving them? Explain.

How can a Christian be salt and light to an unbeliever without being judgmental?

What are your biggest unanswered questions regarding heaven and hell?

questions for action

Do you know where you will be going when you die?

Who do you know who might be on the wrong path? How can you help?

Such was my heart, O God, such
was my heart. . . . It was foul, and
I loved it. I loved the self-destruction,
I loved my fall, not the object for
which I had fallen but my fall itself.
My depraved soul leaped down from
your firmament to ruin. I was seeking
not to gain anything by shameful
means, but shame for its own sake.

—**St. Augustine**

9

the other reason

one final barrier

We have navigated our way through six faith-shaking topics
so far. These barriers are common rocks that have shipwrecked
many people's spiritual voyages. There is no honest way around
them, and we dare not turn back because of them. You and
I must make our own way through the thicket of doubts and
questions in order to keep pursuing Jesus. In your journey,
I hope you find a relevant and inspiring church to connect
with. You may battle through incredible pain and suffering in
your own life and keep going. You might challenge the
hypocrisy around you with courage and integrity. You might
discover the rational credibility of the Christian faith and
defend it to skeptics. You may grasp a deeper understanding

of the relationship between creation and the discoveries of science. You might figure out how to relate to people of other faiths. Maybe you've found the answers you need, or maybe you have a lot more searching to do. If you're ready to move forward with Jesus, be prepared. There is one final barrier.

Some people abandon the narrow path simply because they like the other one better. They enjoy being in charge of their own lives. We might initially give our lives to Jesus and walk his narrow road because it seems like the best option for us. He offers forgiveness and unconditional love. However, the longer we travel down the road, the more we come to realize that Jesus wants to be the Lord of *every* part of our lives. We cannot give him partial access. There are no restricted zones. His intention for us is pure love, and that love over the course of our lives will transform who we are and how we live. His love will dig up the roots of "the other reason" and throw them out. What is the other reason? What is the final barrier? In classical terms, it is called sin.

hard to say good-bye

God is not a concept to which we give intellectual adherence. He is a personal, living being. Jesus is not a mythological example of morality; he is the genuine Son of God. The Holy Spirit is not a feeling or an emotion; he is a real, personal being who is intimately connected with every Christian. With the help of God, we might untangle the rational knots that seem to hold us back from believing in the Bible's message. But this is not enough. We were designed for relationship. Somehow in his mysterious grace, God has arranged it so that we can join in the friendship and love that exists between the Father, Son, and Holy Spirit. We are closer to God than what should be humanly possible. The change that God brings into our lives is in one sense immediate because we are instantly forgiven, reborn, and connected with his Spirit. But in another sense, the change is gradual because it continues over the course of our lives. The transformation begins at the trailhead but continues for many miles.

Jesus wants us to be holy. He wants sin to have no place in our lives. Another way to say this is that he wants us to live for him and not against him. Pretty simple in theory. Pretty brutal in practice. Sin is the deal breaker for some. When Jesus begins to lovingly ask us to rid the filth from our lives, sometimes we'd rather say, "No thanks. I'm going to keep this filth right where it is. I like it. You can't mess with it."

We know sin is wrong, but saying good-bye is painful at times. We can resist Jesus because we'd rather have our own thrills. We can choose the junk food instead of the gourmet meal. We can read the trashy romance novel instead of living the real romance. We can muddle around in mediocrity and lethargy at our own discretion, instead of letting God take us to greatness. The choice is always ours. Unfortunately, the deeper the roots of sin grow into us, the harder they are to unearth.

You might come right to the edge of having faith. You may have no good reason not to follow Jesus. But you can still turn away because of sin. If you do, you must know that you are making a tragic trade. You've given up on life and joy in exchange for addictive lusts that will never satisfy you. Sin leads to death. If you resist Jesus because you like sin too much, at least have enough honor to admit to it. Don't make excuses as to why you don't believe. If you'd rather have sin than Jesus, don't blame it on hypocrites, boring churches, or science.

The irony of sin is that it is always a lie. You're promised happiness and get misery. You taste life and swallow rotten death. You start out in great company and end up alone. Loving anything more than God will disrupt our navigation systems and cause a crash. For some it's money they love most; for others it's their reputation, security, an unhealthy relationship, or sex outside of marriage. Others hold their fears and low self-esteem at the highest place in their hearts; for some it is substance abuse. These sins are like stone-carved idols. They can never deliver on their promises.

light in the kitchen

When I was in seminary, I was in great distress as I tried to find a good definition for sin. My earlier understanding seemed to be inadequate when compared to the complex theologies I encountered. So I sought a better rational formulation. For several months, I floated in a state of spiritual limbo. I knew that if I didn't believe in the biblical concept of sin, then the death and resurrection of Jesus was virtually meaningless. And the rest of my faith would then fall apart piece by piece.

One morning during the midst of this struggle, I was reading at my kitchen table. Suddenly, I was struck with the presence of God. He was with me in the room. I felt overwhelmed. I kneeled and bowed my head to the floor. With tear-filled, closed eyes, God's presence was like a bright light penetrating my soul. The dark corners of my thoughts, my secret actions, and my doubts were all brought into his light. In the light of God, I could see my sin clearly. I could feel it painfully. I needed no definitions. Being near God made it obvious. I knew I was wrong for the first time in a long time. "I'm so sorry," I kept saying over and over. It was a tremendous relief to know my own sin. I knew God would be quick to forgive. The darkness of doubt was lifted, and I felt clean.

Sin does not have to be a barrier between you and God. Its roots don't have to immobilize your progress or drain your vital energy. God's way of living is better than our own plans. When we let go of sin with our hearts and ask God to forgive us with our lips, dynamic change will take place. And we will be unrelenting on the narrow path.

questions for reflection

What sins in your life seem to be holding you back?
Do you love anything or anyone more than you love God?

question for action

How will you deal with your sin so that you can love God better?

Faith is the bird
that sings when
the dawn is
still dark.

—**Rabindranath Tagore**

10

moving forward with life

my story

If you are still reading this book, we have journeyed together for a while now. I am grateful to walk with you on this spiritual pilgrimage. When my faith was collapsing, there were a few people who walked with me as faithful friends. They didn't know where I was headed or if I would ruin myself, but they remained at my side. They patiently listened to my ranting questions. They did not try to fix me. They did not pray for me when I was with them (because I wouldn't let them!). They did not cast me out of their inner circle or call me a heretic. They simply stood strong while I fell apart.

Others became nervous at my faith crisis. They were worried for me, and I think they secretly feared for their own faith.

With sincere hearts, they encouraged me to keep pressing on. These people saw that I was angry and jaded. They watched my previously sure footing start to wobble. They probably prayed for me in the quiet of their bedrooms at night. They waited to see if this new and dangerous path I was walking would turn out OK. And when it did, their faith grew stronger too.

During this crisis, a select few patiently listened and then (metaphorically) slapped me in the face. I am especially thankful for them. They were the sages I sought out, the ones with scars. They had already walked through the valley of the shadow of death and learned to fear no evil. They were the ones who survived the assault of their own doubts. If you looked closely, you could observe a slight limp in their gait because they had wrestled with God. At critical forks in my path, they pointed down one side and said, "If you go here, you'll die." Then they pointed down the other side and said, "If you have the courage to go here, you'll find life."

The chapters in this book are like mile markers in my spiritual journey. After being burned out on boring churches, I discovered that most of the trouble was inside me, not them. I also found a few churches and leaders that changed my perspective. I met pastors who captivated, devastated, and inspired me. I went to a church so alive that I couldn't wait until Sunday morning came around again. I realized how much Jesus loves his church, so I started loving it more too. I even became a pastor.

I transformed pain into motivation. After watching hypocrites cause major damage to the faith of others, I decided to try with God's help to leave a legacy that would honor him and inspire courage in others. After facing suffering in my own life, I learned that God can heal broken hearts and even broken bodies. I would much rather follow the example of Jesus, who was faithful even at great personal sacrifice, than give up and lose at life because of illness, injury, or agony.

After pushing my rationality to its limits, I came to the conclusion that relating to God requires more than pure reason. Faith cannot be bound by the rules of logic because God transcends our abilities to contain and control him. He has established a more humble approach for us, one where he reveals himself to us, and we respond with gratitude. Likewise, my thoughts on evolution have evolved over the last decade. I am sure the world is not as godless as many believe. Good science does not eliminate the existence of God, nor does it eliminate the mystery of the universe. I am eager to learn of both.

After traveling to a few different parts of the world, I have realized that cultures are very different. People relate to the one true God in their own unique ways, but the truth is always one, the same and forever. It can be translated to different languages. It can take different shapes and sizes. But it is not relative. Jesus is still the only hope of the world.

I am thankful for the family, friends, and face slappers who walked with me. But I am even more thankful for God. At the moment when I thought I had it all figured out, he broke me. When I was overzealous and under-wise, he let me bleed with the world's wounded. When I was slipping from the end of my rope, he did not catch me. Instead, he let me fall and break so that my faith could be reforged. When I doubted everything, he stayed face-to-face. When I was throwing punches, he hit harder. When I was wandering in the wrong direction, he was quietly rerouting me back onto the right path. When I gave up, he gave hope. When I was unqualified, he called me forward. When I was jaded, he brought new life.

your story

I said earlier that those who intensely look for God will find him. If we open our hearts, explore with our minds, and surrender our lives, God will certainly show up. When, where, and how? I'm not sure. But he will. Keep searching.

Once you have decided to follow Jesus, never give up. You are among heroes. You are treading the dirt of great ones who have gone before you. Faith was their inspiration. God was their trail guide. They saw a vision of their true home, and they were unyielding to the threats before them. Pain could not crush them. Doubt did not demoralize them. Questions fueled their quests. They trudged through the valley of jaded faith and found life on the other side.

a few traveling tips

find a mentor

Search for someone you respect and set a regular meeting to discuss your spiritual journey.

keep exploring

If you go back to your original list from chapter 2, you can identify the areas of uncertainty you still have. Find a book, article, blog, video, or expert on this topic. Learn more. Pursue the truth. Don't give up at the first sign of doubts.

talk with God

Share your thoughts and feelings with him. Write these conversations in a journal. Pay attention to how God may be responding to you.

connect with a church

You can't be a Christian alone. Keep searching until you find a church; then jump in.

share your journey with a Christian friend

It is important to let other people get close to you, even if they are nervous about your jaded faith. You might be surprised what you learn about others if you open up to them. Christian friends can be a great support, even if they can't totally relate to what you're going through.

pay it forward

When you are strong, help others who are struggling. Be a catalyst to those who have given up. Be a comforter to the brokenhearted. Be a voice of reason to the doubters. Be a caring friend to the lonely. Help them see that there is hope for those who still want to believe.